Parental Involvement
and the Political Principle

Seymour B. Sarason

Parental Involvement and the Political Principle

Why the Existing Governance Structure of Schools Should Be Abolished

Jossey-Bass Publishers • San Francisco

Substantial discounts on bulk quantities of Jossey-Bass books are available to corporations, professional associations, and other organizations. For details and discount information, contact the special sales department at Jossey-Bass Inc., Publishers. (415) 433–1740; Fax (800) 605–2665.

For sales outside the United States, please contact your local Paramount Publishing International Office.

▲TCF Manufactured in the United States of America on Lyons Falls Pathfinder Tradebook. This paper is acid-free and 100 percent totally chlorine-free.

Library of Congress Cataloging-in-Publication Data
Sarason, Seymour Bernard, date.
    Parental involvement and the political principle: why the existing governance structure of schools should be abolished/ Seymour B. Sarason.—1st ed.
      p. cm.—(The Jossey-Bass education series)
    ISBN 0-7879-0054-0
    1. School management and organization—United States.
  2. Education—Parent participation—United States. 3. School boards—United States. 4. Politics and education—United States.
  5. Educational change—United States.   I. Title. II. Series.
LB2805.S267 1995
371.2'00973—dc20
                                    94-33600
                                     CIP

FIRST EDITION
HB Printing   10 9 8 7 6 5 4 3 2 1   *Code 9512*

Contents

For Irma Miller
with my love

Acknowledgments

I am most grateful to my friend, Edward Meyer, for the diverse kinds of help he provided me in writing this book. He has been a source of ideas and encouragement. And, of course, I am grateful to Lisa Pagliaro for her brightness, charm, and friendship, in addition to her ability to read my handwriting.

The Author

Seymour B. Sarason is professor of psychology emeritus in the Department of Psychology and at the Institution for Social and Policy Studies at Yale University. He founded, in 1962, and directed, until 1970, the Yale Psycho-Educational Clinic, one of the first research and training sites in community psychology. He received his Ph.D. degree from Clark University in 1942 and holds honorary doctorates from Syracuse University, Queens College, Rhode Island College, and Lewis and Clark College. He has received an award for distinguished contributions to the public interest and several awards from the divisions of clinical and community psychology of the American Psychological Association, as well as two awards from the American Association on Mental Deficiency.

Sarason is the author of numerous books and articles. His more recent books include *Psychoanalysis, General Custer, and the Verdicts of History and Other Essays on Psychology in the Social Scene* (1994), *You Are Thinking of Teaching: Opportunities, Problems, Realities* (1993), *The Case for Change: Rethinking the Preparation of Educators* (1993), *Letters to a Serious Education President* (1993), *The Predictable Failure of Educational Reform: Can We Change Course Before It's Too Late?* (1990), *The Challenge of Art to Psychology* (1990), and *The Making of an American Psychologist: An Autobiography* (1988). He has made contributions in such fields as mental retardation, culture and personality, projective techniques, teacher training, the school culture, and anxiety in children.

Chapter One

Stating the Problem

The sole purpose of this book is to stimulate discussion about changing the governance (local and state) of schools and school systems. Many before me have made similar pleas, but their efforts did not result in a public discussion, let alone a debate. It was an instance of an idea whose time had not come. Although our educational system has never been without its articulate critics, with rare exceptions those critics accepted the existing governance structure as a given. That is understandable. After all, we have grown up in and have been socialized in that structure, which seemed to have a plausible, indeed self-evident, justification. Words like *governance structure* are concepts or abstractions that have no concrete referents the way words like *teacher, principal, superintendent,* and *board of education* have. You can see and touch a teacher; you cannot do so with a "governance structure"—words denoting not things but rather the allocation, distribution, and uses of power to achieve stated goals for a circumscribed entity like a school or school system. No one in such an entity is in doubt that his or her relationships with others have meaning in terms of the "local" rules and goals of governance, but very few people understand how those relationships are determined by rules and goals of the larger structure (i.e., features not "visible" in those local relationships). We readily assent to the assertion that a parent (or his or her child) has a very incomplete picture and understanding of the structure of school and school system governance. But when I say, as I have in the past, that many, if not most, people in schools have a very incomplete grasp of the governance structure of schools and school

systems, assent is not forthcoming, at least initially. Each individual likes to believe that he or she comprehends the whys, where-
fores, and details of governance until they realize two things: how
frequently they are puzzled by and resentful of the ways in which
power is allocated and used by those "elsewhere" in the governance
structure, and how frequently the formal description of how things
are done and why diverges from how things are "really" done and
why. The formal description of a governance structure should never
be confused with its informal characteristics, and that is true for the
entity we call a family, a school, and any other recognized formal
organization. Just as we know that having power does not equate
with having influence, the formal governance structure should not
be equated with the informal one, which is what so many of us do.

Someone once described the university as a form of legally sanctioned anarchy, a quip too readily seized upon by those who have
no comprehension of the formal governance structure of the modal
university and who are surprised when faculty complain that far
from being anarchic the university is increasingly becoming bureau-
cratized in ways inimical to the purposes of university governance.
My point here is not to defend the university but rather to emphasize that because a "governance structure" is not visible the way faculty members are, it is all too easy to reach oversimple conclusions
about the nature of the structure and, no less important, about how
its changing features impact on its informal ones. When I have discussed the complexity and problems of the governance structure of
our public schools with university colleagues, a frequent reaction is
"The governing structure of our public schools is a model of sim-
plicity and clarity compared to the Byzantine one of the university."
When on occasion I have tried to describe university governance
structure to public school educators, their first response is one of
surprise, if not disbelief, and then the question "Then why is it that
university people have a far higher level of job satisfaction, and far
more public respect, than public school personnel enjoy, even
though, as you say, the average salary for teachers in Connecticut

[highest in the country] is above that of assistant professors and many beginning associate professors, and you may be a member of a university faculty for ten years without being given tenure?" That is a very good question for which the answer is truly complex, and I shall not attempt to discuss it in this book (for which the reader should thank God for big favors). But the importance of the question for my present purposes lies in what is implicit and explicit in it. What is explicit is that both educators and the public are dissatisfied with what schools are and do or do not do, a degree of dissatisfaction in comparison to which dissatisfaction with the university seems minuscule indeed. What is implicit in the question is that educators and the public sense that the governance structure of our public schools somehow has to be *part* of the problem. I say "sense" and "somehow" because dissatisfaction with our schools is directed to so many of its features that appear to be visible and measurable that the role of what is not visible, namely governance structure, rarely comes into clear focus. The pejorative epithet "bureaucratic" I do not regard as illuminating because it suggests that with less bureaucracy and better selection of personnel the situation would be vastly improved, a suggestion that leaves governance structure intact and undiscussed, a kind of organizational tinkering or "administrative restructuring" that has the sole virtue of appearing to be doing *something, anything,* to alter what is recognized as an unacceptable state of affairs. These are always well-intentioned efforts. I do not say that to sugarcoat my criticism but rather as a form of compliment. Over the course of my professional career I have spent thousands of hours in classrooms and in meetings with educators. If anything is justified from my experience it is the conclusion that although educators correctly indict governance structure as a major part of the problem—an indictment they too often will not articulate in public forums—they not only are puzzled by what to do about it, but, especially in the case of teachers, they react to the usual tinkering with "Here we go again." And in the quiet of their nights a surprising number of administrators agree with them.

Challenging an existing governance structure is one thing; changing it is quite another matter. For example, the *New York Times* this spring carried a long article discussing, in part, why a traditional aspect of university governance (departmental structure) may be in the process of transformation:

> Human DNA can best be understood or studied as "a work of literature." That, at least, is the contention of Robert Pollack, a professor of biological sciences at Columbia University who has just unveiled the theory in his book "Signs of Life."
>
> Scholars and scientists will recognize Professor Pollack's thesis as an example of one of the hottest trends in current academic life: interdisciplinary studies. At campuses across the country, biology is merging with physics and chemistry, anthropology is borrowing from literary theory and feminist studies, economics is mixing with cognitive psychology and biospheric studies, and political science is absorbing mathematics, molecular biology and environmental studies.
>
> "The boundaries between disciplines are becoming blurred," said Sheldon Hackney, the chairman of the National Endowment for the Humanities. "We've reached the point in the study of American history where you can't tell the difference between what the sociologists, the political scientists and the historians are doing."

A Basic Transformation

Of course, interdisciplinary studies are not new. In the 1930's, for example, undergraduates at Yale University could major in an interdisciplinary program called "History, the Arts and Letters." But in the past, scholars would leap academic borders to borrow a skill to solve a specific problem and then retreat. Today, they interact with such intensity that their disciplines themselves frequently become transformed.

In current interdisciplinary studies, explained Colin Lucas, dean of the graduate division of social sciences at the University of

Chicago, "you don't just acquire a technique, but new forms appear within your discipline, modifying the discipline itself."

Educational administrators say that young faculty members and students are propelling the trend, which may also transform the university, abolishing outmoded disciplines, creating new ones and developing ways to attack problems from more than one direction rather than compartmentalizing knowledge.

"We're beginning to recognize that God did not create the universe according to the departmental structure of our research universities," said John A. Armstrong, former director of research at I.B.M. and a visiting lecturer at the Massachusetts Institute of Technology.

Some professors look upon the trend with dismay. Harvey Mansfield, a professor of political philosophy at Harvard, said interdisciplinary studies "allow professors who don't want to pursue a normal and presumably difficult path to make a success of their unstudied opinions."

But the continued surge of interdisciplinary studies is not without a major obstacle: the departmental structure of American colleges and universities. Departments determine raises, promotions and tenure, and many are notoriously unsympathetic toward faculty members who work outside their disciplines.

Donald McCloskey, a professor of economics and history at the University of Iowa, has written several books arguing that economic writing has much in common with fiction. But because of such academic trespassing, his professional colleagues say, he has not been invited to teach at a top-tier university.

"The system rewards you for becoming boring," Professor Winn of Michigan said. "If a specialist in the Victorian novel writes a book on film, even a brilliant book, his colleagues will say he's 'all over the place' and not doing his job."

Others prefer to retain the current departmental structure.

"Interdisciplinary work depends on having the disciplines," said Professor Arjun Appadurai, an anthropologist at the University of Chicago who is studying what he calls postnational global allegiances.

"It's like managing a portfolio of stocks. You don't want to become fossilized, and you don't want to be overtaken by fashion. You have to strike a balance."

Still others believe that the interdisciplinary studies movement is merely a transitional stage toward a radically different university.

Interdisciplinary study is only "a temporary effort to get at a greater interconnectedness," said Ralph Cohen, a professor of English at the University of Virginia and director of the Commonwealth Center for Literary and Cultural Change.

"Ultimately, the whole structure of the university must be changed," he said, "but that's a job for the next century" ["Academic Disciplines," 1994].

The proponents for transformation in governance structure would agree that God did not create the university departmental structure, an argument with which all who challenge the existing governance structure of *our schools* would agree. The opponents of transformation do not bring God into the picture but have no doubt that He looks approvingly on the departmental structure, just as those who oppose changes in governance structure of our public schools do not doubt God's approval of the way things are. The significance to me of the article is that, in contrast to the silence of the public school educational community, the issue of changes in university governance is at least being posed. I was in the university for over forty years, during which time I heard many colleagues publicly challenge and indict the existing governance structure. I have never heard any educator in a school system do that even though privately they were in no doubt that governance structure was part of the problem and could never be part of the solution. Their silence speaks volumes, to me at least, of how the existing governance structure effectively inhibits the expression of views.

This book does not begin but ends with an argument for abolishing boards of education and for delineating and examining the universe of alternatives to existing school governance. Leaving that argument toward the end was not a matter of aesthetics. The fact is that I did not come to see the bedrock importance of a changed structure until I had thought through the necessity and wisdom of the political principle: when you are going to be affected, directly or indirectly, by a decision, you should stand in *some* relationship to the decision-making process. Once the implications of that became belatedly clear to me, I then saw that among the most effective barriers to accepting and acting consistently with that principle were our ways of defining the assets and deficits of people, *barriers as strong between the different layers of the school hierarchy as they are between that hierarchy and parent-community groups.* One of those barriers, of course, is in the form of rigid boundaries professionals erect to insure that "outsiders" (who may be other kinds of professionals) remain outsiders. I am no mindless antiprofessional (although I have sometimes been seen as such). But neither am I blind to how the spirit or ethos of professionalism is a source of serious problems. In this regard, I do not think that readers who are educators will have any basis for concluding that I am singling out educators for criticism. I go to some lengths to note that the occupational hazards of professionalism are by no means peculiar to educators.

Having clarified for myself the importance of the political principle, the issues surrounding how we define the assets and deficits of parents, and the role of professionalism, it became obvious to me that taking the political principle seriously was impossible in the existing governance structure. It introduced a complexity, a "messiness," a surface "inefficiency" for which the existing governance structure was utterly inadequate, indeed lethal. So, that is why this book is organized as it is: a kind of chronicle of the steps I had to take in order to see what I should have seen a long time ago: the governance structure of our schools has to be changed if we stand any chance at all of preventing a further deterioration in the quality of the experience of children *and* of educators.

The reader may feel disappointed that I do not present a blueprint for a new governance structure. The reasons I do not present a plan are several. The first is that the problem is so complex, so embedded in our national history, so full of dilemmas and potential booby traps, so unexamined a problem, that I frankly felt overwhelmed and unprepared, although I was not devoid of ideas. The second reason is that it is not a problem for *an* individual but rather one literally demanding the minds and passions of a group of knowledgeable individuals (not necessarily "experts") who however they may vary in numerous ways have in common the stance that a new governance structure needs to be developed. That is why I use the constitutional convention of 1787, where there was agreement that the Articles of Confederation had to be superseded, as a model for what a presidentially-congressionally appointed commission should be asked to do, with the goal of making school governance a focus of national discussion and debate. Unless and until that kind of discussion takes place, I find no basis whatsoever for expecting that our schools will improve; indeed I predict they will get worse, a prediction I have been making on other grounds for many years. I take no satisfaction in having an excellent track record for predicting failure of all past efforts to improve schools generally. Indeed, the third reason for calling for a "constitutional convention" on school governance is that I fear that if it does not take place, the dismantling of our public school system will pick up steam, a possibility that a disillusioned public will not strongly oppose and that some vocal, tunnel-vision ideologues will greet with joy. There is a difference between changing schools and dismantling them. I know I run the risk of being perceived as a senior citizen who indulges predictions of gloom and doom. To those who may so perceive me may I express the hope that they will at least acknowledge that I am not nostalgically calling for a return to an earlier state of grace that did not exist. On the contrary, over the decades I have been chronicling something akin to a fool's paradise, and others now and in the past have said similar things.

Changing governance structure does not by any means guarantee desirable outcomes. There is a prior question the answer to which should inform changes in governance structure. What is the overarching criterion by which we should judge the efficacy of schooling? Please note that I say *criterion* and not *criteria*. There are and should be several criteria, but there is one I consider the most important because if you take it seriously, and few have, it affects how you will perceive every other criterion. I predict that no reader will disagree with the singular importance I attach to that criterion, but I also predict that some readers will be troubled by the scope of the implications that criterion has for governance structure and a lot more. Some readers, I have no doubt, will conclude that those implications are so vast that the thought of taking them seriously should be put in the category of pie-in-the-sky musings and fantasies—to which I can only say that we need those musings far more than the mud-in-your-face situation we are in today. We are used to hearing that when mountain climbers are asked why they feel compelled or dream about climbing Mount Everest, they reply, "Because it is there," a challenge to human courage and ambition. Our social world does not change because so few people are able to scale Mount Everest. But our social world has changed and will continue to change in unsatisfactory ways if the number of our children who do not meet the overarching criterion I discuss remains minuscule and even appears to be decreasing. In no way do I suggest that all students will or can meet that criterion if educators and the general public take that criterion seriously. In the realm of human affairs there are no solutions in the sense that four divided by two is a solution; there are only approximations. What we have now is an approximation of defeat and that approximation is in part, but a very important part, a consequence of a governance structure that whatever its early virtues may have been are no longer evident or reclaimable.

In Philip Roth's hilarious *Portnoy's Complaint* the central character, after countless hours on the analytic couch of whining and indicting this or that person or event and the world generally, is asked by his analyst, "So, shall we begin?" (i.e., "Are you *finally* ready to confront *yourself?*"). Confronting myself was the precondition for writing this book. If it helps the reader confront the self, I can ask for no more. If it does not, I apologize for wasting your time; there are other "analysts" who will bring you gladder, easier tidings. I do not say that with any intention of being humorous. There is too much at stake for that. So, shall we begin?

Chapter Two

Considerations of Power

It is quite fashionable to proclaim the necessity and desirability of parent involvement in our public schools. Such proclamations have the ring of virtue, inclusion, and a democratic ethos. If this affirmation of value and goal is well intentioned, the fact is that it is too often empty rhetoric, and when it is not empty rhetoric, the actions they give rise to are more like shadow boxing or, less frequently but fatefully, naive in the extreme about the problems they will engender. That, I know, will sound like a harsh judgment, a pessimistic note about an aspect of educational reform that seems as virtuous as motherhood and patriotism. As a way of self-defense, I ask you to ponder this question: why is it that the call for parental involvement was hardly audible before the 1960s? Hundreds (really thousands) of articles and books have addressed that question, and in the course of these pages I shall discuss some of the answers given. Here I wish only to note that one answer was in two parts: our schools were inadequate in diverse ways, and blame had to be assigned to the educators responsible for the schools but who seemed incapable of changing them. Let us not be detained here by the appropriateness (in direction and depth) of the criticisms. The point is that the call for parental involvement was an explicit challenge to the status quo in regard to the use and distribution of power in the formulation of educational policy and in educational practice. If the challenge was explicit, it was quite murky in content. On the one hand, those calling for parental involvement were by no means clear about the foci of such involvement, its means, forums, and specific goals; on the other hand, embattled educators seemed willing, so to speak, to roll with the punch if only because what was being called for had the characteristics of an ink blot; that is, they interpreted the challenge as significant but in no basic way a threat to their customary autonomy. It is fair to say that neither side recognized that however explicit the criticisms, the *implicit* logic of the criticisms could be revolutionary *depending on the outcome of whatever forms parental involvement took*. I use the word *revolutionary* advisedly because if the outcomes led nowhere, educationally speaking, it was likely to result in further blame of educators and a call for more parental involvement but now on a legal-legislative basis. This, in fact, is what happened in some states, and especially in some of our urban areas where power relationships have been altered.

Whatever other characteristics societal and institutional revolutions may have, they share the characteristics of altering traditional power relationships. But with few exceptions, of which the American revolution is the most notable, revolutions (institutional and societal) tend to devour their makers, not only because the course of revolutions is far from controllable and predictable but because revolutionary agendas are far more in the nature of sloganeering than they are a recognition of the complexity of the issues surrounding alterations of power. In my opinion, parental involvement as a rallying cry has been a mixture of rhetoric and sloganeering, unassailably well intentioned and justifiable at the same time that it lacked and still lacks content, scope, and sensitivity to what is at stake. And what is at stake is not power in and of itself but the concrete ways by which alterations of power will in turn alter the ecology of classrooms, schools, and their surrounding communities. That latter alteration is in no way guaranteed by the fact that parents seek, attain, or are given power through legislation. Service in the power of what goals? It is a complete cop-out to say that power is in the service of improving the quality of education because that begs the question of what you mean by education and quality. Since the call for parental involvement derived from the perception that the quality of education was low, that call should have been accompanied by an attempt to define the concept of quality education *and* to indicate how parental involvement would improve quality. That attempt, for all practical purposes, was absent. Unless, of course, you equated the raising of achievement test scores with quality education, an equation that was as narrow and mischievous as it was impossible to solve *unless alterations in power dramatically changed the culture of schools in specifiable ways.* But those ways have never been specified by advocates of parental involvement. That is why beginning in the late sixties I predicted, orally and in print, that parental involvement would have no discernible positive effects, certainly not a general effect although one could point to a school here and a school there where such effects seemed to have been obtained. Generally speaking, parental involvement can claim no victories, unless shadow boxing is a victory. There is far more compelling evidence, again from our urban areas, that parental involvement has been productive of conflict, not of a problem-solving process.

Where there is a change in power relationships one expects conflict. In such a situation conflict is as predictable as the rising sun. And, yet, I have seen many instances, and have read about many more, where initiating parental involvement was approached with the attitude that good intentions are a universal solvent for difficult predictable problems, an attitude based on a psychology of human and institutional behavior unrealistic in the extreme. If conflict is predictable, it does not mean that one is without means to lessen (not to eliminate) its unproductive consequences (i.e., to take preventive actions). But to take preventive actions is possible only if one has grasped the complexity of the task and adopts a realistic time perspective. That has not been in the picture in regard to parental involvement. So, for example, for a state legislature to mandate some form of parental involvement without explicitly recognizing, recommending, and supporting preventive courses of action is, unfortunately, an example of the road to hell paved with good intentions.

Earlier I said that the American revolution was an exception to the fate of most revolutions. The instructive fact is that it came perilously close to being no exception because that revolution was in its own way powered by the sloganlike "Taxation without representation is tyranny." It was not powered by anything resembling a clear picture of what should be the basis of the new nation. It would be more correct to say that it was assumed that the new basis would not be all that different from prerevolutionary days. That is, each of the thirteen states would be, for all practical purposes, autonomous with a central government having little power to influence each state, to weld the states into a nation, to overcome vested regional interests for overarching national purposes, and to forge a sense of community and purpose that could withstand external threats to the security of the fledgling country. The Articles of Confederation had some of the characteristics of a blueprint for disaster. It did not take long for that possibility to be recognized, and that recognition started one of the most sustained, searching, analytical, concrete discussion-controversies in human history, not the least of its virtues being the exposure of how superficial, incomplete, and dangerous had been the thinking that gave rise to the Articles of Confederation, well intentioned but very flawed.

So what should be done? As the reader knows, each state sent a representative to a constitutional convention that met for several months in hot, steamy Philadelphia. The proceedings of that convention are a reminder of what is possible when a group of people—aware of the history of power, conscious of its positive and negative uses, intent on preventing its abuses, crystal clear about values and goals, unafraid of being specific and concrete (indeed, dotting as many i's and crossing as many t's as possible)—confront the inadequacies of what is and the realities of a new alteration in power relationships. The American Constitution is the opposite of sloganeering or an example of pious generalizations. I like to characterize the constitutional convention of 1787 as an instance undergirded by this stance: "If the road to hell is paved with good intentions, as indeed it is, our job is to come up with a map that will guide us to more productive roads."

In regard to our schools and parental involvement we are in the Articles of Confederation phase: vested interests understand-ably intent on maintaining the status quo, a lack of clarity (to be charitable) about means and ends, a surface appearance of unity and hope beneath which is confusion and anger, and an unwill-ingness or inability to face up to the fact that despite all that has been tried in the post–World War II era to improve our schools, the quality of education, however defined, remains what it has been or is getting worse. If, as I predict and fear, nothing will change or the situation will worsen, then our schools will, like the states under the Articles of Confederation, be prey to "foreign forces," which in this case will be the larger society saying, "No more. Let the dismantling process begin."

This book has several purposes of which the most important is to convince the reader that the principles justifying parental involvement lead one to opportunities and dilemmas far beyond what is conventionally meant by parental involvement. Those prin-ciples have logical, percolating consequences that I attempt to sketch. A second purpose is to indicate that if we take these princi-ples seriously, we are faced with two very contrasting courses of action: that of repair and that of prevention, and in the "real world" those two types of action will be taken at the same time. But in that same real world—as history repeatedly tells us—the preventive course of action will be glossed over, at best, and ignored, at worst. That, it is needless to say, is all the more reason for me again (as in previous of my books) to emphasize that neglect of the preventive orientation diminishes the potential benefits to be derived from the principles justifying parental involvement. What I say on this score will be put by some readers in the category of "pie-in-the-sky" mus-ings, or an indulgence of wishful thinking, or a symptom of a more malignant psychological tendency. To those readers I say what I said earlier: I have been 100 percent correct in predicting that nostrums, in the past and in the present, would have little or no positive, general consequences precisely because they have been exclusively efforts at repair. A third purpose of this book is to suggest to educators that their dissatisfaction with the fruits of their efforts, their low level of morale, derive in large measure from their reactive stance (i.e., as a group their actions contain no hint of a proactive stance). That is but another way of saying that leadership in the educational community has been unimaginative, timid, parochial, and unconscionably traditional. Those are adjectives that were frequently used by the early proponents of parental involvement who were puzzled by and resentful of the reaction of educators to what then were very modest proposals. Over time the puzzlement has decreased, and the resentment has increased.

An analogy may be helpful here. Up until 1993 the response of the medical community to the idea of national health insurance was predictably swift and negative. The reaction of that community gave one the impression that national health insurance would be a national catastrophe. What went remarkably unnoticed should have been obvious: that community presented no alternative program to deal with the brute fact of an inequitable availability of medical services, quantitatively and qualitatively. This was blatantly the case when in 1965 the Medicare proposal came before the Congress. The American Medical Association fought the initial proposal tooth and nail, and its teeth and nails were quite sharp. As a result, the legislation did not pass until it was modified to protect the autonomy of physicians and, predictably, opened up new vistas for increased income. Although it was claimed that the final legislation would improve the quality of care older citizens received, the evidence was not forthcoming. On the contrary, the nursing home scandals and kindred entrepreneurial hanky-panky suggested (and still suggests) otherwise. The medical community's victory was, however, a Pyrrhic one and for a reason of which they were not but could (and should) have been aware. Yes, they maintained their autonomy and increased their incomes, but they *forever* put themselves under the control of an external agency (the federal government) that, as Medicare costs surged, steadily decreased the scope of that autonomy at the same time it increased paperwork mightily. That was the price paid for being clear about what they were against and unable to come up with their own program that met crying societal needs. And today (1994) when national health insurance has been in principle universally accepted and its outlines can be glimpsed, the medical community is in a state of disarray as never before, with physicians, hospitals, HMOs, and insurance companies vying with each other, fearful for their very existence.

The educational community is fast approaching the current condition of the medical one. The public is dissatisfied with our schools, and educators are perceived as resistant to change and concerned only with money and control, and lacking a leadership capable of changing educational practices, organizational characteristics, *and the relationships with the larger community*. I italicize those words to emphasize a point I shall be stressing in later pages: parents are no longer the only "external" group vitally concerned with what happens in school; politicians, legislators, the entities we call state and federal government, leaders of minority groups, business executives, and others seek to get into the act on the basis of their different purposes, agendas, and constituencies. As someone said, "If they are not taking dead aim at our schools, let us not forget that they have guns and they are in the rehearsal phase." It is in no way to downplay the significance of parent involvement to say that parents are but one group with a stake in educational improvement.

My hold on reality is not so tenuous as to prevent me from entertaining the possibility that the picture I have painted may be too grim and that our schools will "muddle through" their current travails, relatively intact in terms of their encapsulated cultural-organizational features, except, of course, for cosmetic changes that confirm the maxim that the more things change the more they remain the same. The fact is that this book is not being written as a venture in educational forecasting, although that feature is not absent, but as a way of stating and pursuing the implications of a *political* principle without which adherence to a democratic ethos is no more than wordplay. It is a principle implied in Churchill's quip that "democracy is the most inefficient form of government except for all others that have been tried." It is a principle easy to state but extraordinarily difficult for people to respect in action. So let us begin in the next chapter to try to understand why what we want for ourselves we have trouble accepting and respecting in others. As Churchill's quip implies, when you accept and respect that want in others, life is never smooth. It is not that you have opened a can of worms but a can containing dilemmas and opportunities in equal proportions, assuming you are lucky or God is on your side.

Chapter Three

Sources of Resistance

The political principle justifying parental involvement is that when decisions are made affecting you or your possessions, you should have a role, a voice in the process of decision making. You may call it a principle, a value, a right. It is not a *formal* rule, law, or a contract mutually agreed upon. It is a principle undergirding and embodied in our legal and political systems. How or when it should be reflected in relationships or practice depends on circumstances. It is not a principle without justifiable exceptions. So, for example, if a group of your friends or relatives decide to honor you with a surprise party—an occasion that is intended to affect you and stay in your memory—they will not include you in the decision. You do not, of course, resent having no voice in the decision. But take the situation where a friend invites you to a dinner party in his or her home and when you get there you find that your host also had invited someone whom your friend knew you cordially disliked or, worse yet, with whom you had severed relationships. You would direct your anger at your host for not giving you the opportunity to decide whether to come or not. You will justly say your host was insensitive, by which you mean that your host made a unilateral decision that would negatively affect you. What if your host did not know that you disliked the other invitee? You would expect that person to say that if he or she had known, a unilateral decision would not have been made.

These are, clearly, nonmomentous examples, which is why they were chosen to make the point that in the relationships we label friendship, well-intended, unilateral decisions may not be in our best interest. But, one could ask, why are these trivial instances illustrations of the *political* principle that is concerned with uses and allocations of *power*, more specifically, relationships in which participants possess different types and degrees of power (e.g., parent and child, teacher and child, supervisor and staff, Congress and the president, a state and the federal government)? The point is that power is not absent between friends but rather that friends have implied equal power; that is, power is not on the interpersonal agenda. The termination of and alterations in friendship frequently occur because of the perception that one of the friends has violated equality in the balance of power.

The call for and the predictable consequences of parental involvement in school matters are not comprehensible apart from the fact that *in regard to the child in the school parents and educators* were unequal in the possession and exercise of power. Yes, educators had always recognized that parents have a legitimate vested interest in what happens to their children in school, but that did not mean to educators that that interest should be formally accompanied by the power to influence how schools and classrooms are structured and run, the choice of curriculum, selection of teachers and other personnel, and so forth. Those matters were off-limits; they were the concern and responsibility of the professional educators. And for a long time that was that; no serious challenge to the status quo was mounted. The opening challenge was the 1954 Supreme Court desegregation decision, the significance of which was initially less in the fact that the plaintiff was a parent than in the more obvious fact that there would be an external force influencing *and* monitoring educational decision making. It was a force more powerful than the powers of educational decision makers (i.e., the latter *had* to comply with the decision, no ifs, ands, or buts). It was predictable that this instance of a legally sanctioned, unilateral decision would meet resistance from certain groups and regions. That is what almost always happens when a "superior power" acts unilaterally toward a less powerful person or agency (i.e., the latter resents having had no voice in a decision altering the style of their existence).

Generally speaking, the educational community was very slow to sense the less obvious implications of that decision; there were many individuals (black and white, parents and others) who would be watching schools to see and judge how seriously, speedily, and effectively school people would change policies and practices to be in accord with the judicial decision that by its very nature was a *national* decision. And, as we know, "seeing and judging" became rather quickly an insistence on the part of parents and others in the community that they be part of the decision-making, policy formulation process. It is an understatement to say that educators were unprepared for the challenge to their power and its exercise. It is not an understatement to say that the preparation of educators was (and still is) woefully deficient in regard to the theories and history of power, its uses and allocation, moral dilemmas, and, perhaps most fateful, the predictable psychological consequences in those who are in relationships of unequal power. It was unpreparedness guaranteeing conflict and led to "parental involvement" becoming a rallying cry giving expression to resentment, anger, and militancy.

The 1954 decision started a train of events in the center of which was the issue of power—who had it and abused it, who should have it but did not. It was a train whose first stop was the station called the sizzling sixties. The long and short of it is that the 1954 decision and its immediate aftermath became a part of a widespread challenge to every major societal institution: churches; the government and the political establishment; business (especially big business); the military and the police; primary, secondary schools, and colleges and universities; and what is suggested by the advice that "You can't trust anyone over thirty." If anything was clear in those days—and few things were clear—it was that these institutions were being accused of aggrandizing power, unilateral, authoritarian decision making, and a gross insensitivity to the needs and rights of society in general and their different constituencies in particular. The timing and force of the call for parental involvement has to be seen in the context of an era in which challenges to power were directed to and far beyond schools, especially in urban areas. And it is important to note that the term "parental involvement" was (is) misleadingly narrow because in regard to schools the call was for "community control" and "community participation." The word *control* was used advisedly, because its proponents meant what they said: drastically to change the balance of power between community and educators.

It is beyond my purposes to say more about the origins of the call for parental involvement. I trust that what I have sketched helps the reader understand how several strands of events combined to make parent-community involvement an issue, a force, and a response to the perceived inadequacies of our schools. It is not an issue that will go away; it is safe to assume that its force will increase. As I said earlier, several states have formally mandated some form of parental involvement, and many school districts have also supported some form of involvement. I shall have more to say about these measures later in this book. Let us in the rest of this chapter pursue the role of motivation of educators in accepting or rejecting the political principle.

A story is appropriate here. It was in the late sixties that I was asked by a suburban school system to meet once a week for ten weeks with elementary school teachers as a forum to discuss matters of practical importance in the classroom. My role was less as a workshop leader and more as a moderator. The first five sessions went well in that a lot of strong feelings and conflicting and conflictful stances got expressed and discussed. One of the themes that came up with heat and regularity is contained in the question I asked early in the sixth session:

I have been reviewing past meetings as a result of which I want to ask a question. Imagine that the board of education asks you to choose between two proposals. The first is that your salary is

increased by a thousand dollars next year. The second is that you
never again have to meet with a parent. Am I wrong to expect that
you would have trouble making your choice?

The nervous, anxious laughter that greeted my question was
indicative of the obvious ambivalence they had previously expressed to parents in this affluent community. I should hasten to
say that, as a group, these were bright, decent, likable, committed
individuals. But in dealing with parents they found them intrusive
and difficult, too quick to offer advice and criticism about matters
the teachers thought them to be uninformed. As one teacher put
it, "Some parents approach me with a chip on their shoulders,
unrespectful of what I know, what I do, or why. And before I know
it, we are talking past each other." Another teacher said, "If some
of my parents talked to their child's pediatrician the way they talk
to me, he probably would tell them to go elsewhere." Still another
teacher said, "When I tell some parents what they can and should
do to help their children, it is as if they think I am trying to cut
back on what I do."

It would be unfair to say that these teachers were, so to speak,
antiparents (i.e., wishing that they would go away and stay away).
What was nettlesome to them was when parents, directly or indirectly, challenged their professional knowledge and practices, and
sometimes the scope of their authority. *That response is not peculiar
to educators; it is a response quite characteristic of those in all of the professions.* It is both incorrect and unjust to single out educators in this
respect. However you define a professional, that person's training
makes clear that there are *boundaries* of responsibility into which
"outsiders" should not be permitted to intrude. Those boundaries are
intended to define and protect the power, authority, and decision
making derived from formal training and experience. Conflicts on
this score are by no means only between the professional and non-
professional; if anything, the conflicts between different kinds of professionals have been more frequent and no less heated. Someone

once remarked that animals are not professionals, but both share the characteristic of brooking no invasion of their turfs.

It is unrealistic to expect that a profession will, without external pressure, be motivated to take the initiative to include outsiders in its customary decision-making ways. It is no less unrealistic to expect that when the external pressure is strong and insistent, conflict is avoidable. That is small balm to participants in the conflict, who tend to see it as a zero-sum game: what *they* win, *we* lose. Nor is it reassuring to the participants to know, as it is quite knowable today, that their particular conflict is no different from that of other professions whose powers are being challenged by outsiders on the basis of the political principle. Nowhere is this more clear than in physician-patient relationships. It used to be that physicians unilaterally decided what course of action was best and when for the patient. In the best circumstances that course of action was arrived at after the physician had considered the universe of possible actions and the safety and dangers of each, an internal, cognitive process not shared with the patient. "Second opinions" were rarely recommended. Doctor knew best! It was the rare patient (parent) who felt secure enough to interrogate or challenge the wisdom or logic of physician's (educator's) thinking, let alone to insist on a second opinion. That type of relationship began to be challenged on the basis of the political principle at about the same time that educators began to be challenged on the same principle by parent-community forces. And it was at the same time that the political principle became part of environmental protection legislation. Those who would be affected by a proposed highway, or dump waste, or building complex, and more, had to have a voice in the final decision; that is, the professional planners could not plan in a social vacuum.

The point here is not that because the political principle is, so to speak, in the air, that the educator should succumb to it. That, as I indicated, has not and is not happening. Controversy and struggle are unavoidable. The point is rather that the educator, *any* professional, has to come to grips with where he or she stands about the *legitimacy* of the principle, *independent* of possible actions that may flow from the principle. In other words, that person is faced with two struggles: the internal struggle about legitimacy of the principle, and then the one about how to handle the consequences of accepting or rejecting it. Accepting the principle "solves" one problem and brings in its wake a host of problems around actions consistent with that principle. Rejecting the principle also is a form of solution, but it, too, leaves one with thorny problems about how to deal with those who are pressuring for parent-community involvement. Each is an instance of problem creation through problem solution. It goes with the territory. In any event, in some ultimate sense the most important question confronting the educator is where he or she stands in regard to the political principle.

A story is relevant here. I came to know well a school principal whose youngest child had a mystifying illness requiring an array of diagnostic procedures and several hospitalizations. He and his wife were upset and angry about many things: the paucity of information given them, puzzlement about who was "on top of the case," the unwillingness or inability of medical and auxiliary personnel to listen to (let alone to follow) the advice of the parents about how to handle *this* child, and resentment, to put it mildly, about being treated as anxious, intrusive ignoramuses. To someone like me who has spent a fair amount of time in and around medical-hospital settings, what the principal related was not an unfamiliar story. But this was a principal who in his own bailiwick saw parents through the lens of professionalism; that is, parents were to be shown respect and given an opportunity to express their opinions, but that in no way meant that what parents thought and felt should determine what he or his teachers decided was the best way to proceed, educationally speaking. He had no trouble identifying parents who were demanding and intrusive (by his lights), parents whom he sought to placate without violating the boundaries of his "professionalism," which meant that he had more than a few parents who viewed him as he and his wife viewed most of those dealing with his sick child.

All of us, like the principal, are not noted for clarity about principles, examining their applicability across situations and problems, and acting consistently in regard to the principles. But if we indubitably have our imperfections—and no one has ever doubted that assertion—are we not obligated to be more humble, or at least more self-critical, about the rigidity of the boundaries we erect around our profession? If stone walls do not good neighbors make, neither do rigid professional boundaries. I said earlier that the first task of the educator is to determine where he or she stands in regard to the political principle independent of its implications for concrete action. I would like to add to that task a subtask: to determine, on the basis of personal experience, how you viewed the political principle when you were the "outsider" trying to get an "insider professional" to take your ideas, feelings, and recommended actions seriously. It is one thing to accept or reject the political principle in the abstract; it is quite another thing to do so on the basis of experience in diverse professional-nonprofessional relationships.

Generally speaking, educators are aware of the political principle but it is not a self-scrutinizing awareness, nor is it one about which they feel sufficiently secure to express openly. It is as if they know that they are under attack, that they are not respected or even liked as much as they feel they should be, and if they were to say out loud what they say to and among themselves, the attack would gain force. They avoid public discussion of the principle except to say (sometimes) in the most general, inoffensive, and unrevealing ways that *of course* parents are vital to the education process, without implying that that affirmation of principle requires some alteration in existing power relationships. So, for example, the Connecticut section of the *New York Times* carried an interview with the president of the Connecticut Education Association to which 28,000 of the state's 36,300 teachers belong ("Evaluating [and Defending] Teachers," 1994). In the course of the interview is the following:

Q. Is there a widening gulf between teachers and parents?

A. If I talk to prospective teachers I tell them there are certain conditions that go with this job. One is that there are people who believe you are not earning your keep, you can never do enough. For many children you will be successful but there will be people who say you did not meet the needs of their child. There are people who when you have their children in your school will advocate for the school. They want small classes and the best for their children and when they leave they no longer have a vested interest. These are the conditions of employment.

I think as teachers we do the best that we can. If there are those who are not doing the best that they can then we ought not to have them there. Someone should take care of that. Someone who is paid that administrative fee.

It is noteworthy that this official does not answer the question, although in his reply there and elsewhere in the interview he conveys the impression that teachers feel embattled and misunderstood. In no way does he ever suggest that *some* of what critics say *may* have validity, or that if parents and others had a role in educational policy and decisions, they would better understand why educators think and practice as they do. At one point he says that in Connecticut "[w]e ought not to be bemoaning the fact that teacher salaries are the highest in the country. We ought to be saying you pay for what you get." That is a strange statement in two respects. First, if Connecticut teachers are the highest paid in the country, why are so many citizens dissatisfied with what they feel they are getting? Second, there is no evidence whatsoever that increasing salaries increases educational outcomes, a fact that bewilders both citizens and educators. Indeed, I have no doubt that his statement increased the gulf between educators and "outsiders." In brief, this educator had the opportunity to state and discuss the political principle but did not do so, leaving the reader with the impression that the political principle does not deserve discussion. I drew the conclusion that he knew full well the significance of the principle but that if he stated his position—leave things as they are—it would not, to indulge understatement, be greeted warmly; the gulf would widen. The point here is *not* if and how the political principle should be implemented but rather that it demands discussion, that it should be on and not under the table, that it is an issue that will not go away, that if undiscussed will ultimately be "solved" by legislative fiat, a process not noted for its efficacy.

I said earlier that when the political principle comes to the fore, conflict is unavoidable. But there is conflict and there is conflict. What we should seek to avoid, for as long as possible, is conflict solely or largely around power, its allocations and uses, conflict in which if one side "wins," the other "loses," the type of conflict the consequences of which are too often self-defeating for all participants. We like to think of ourselves as pragmatic; that is, we judge our intentions and goals by how well our actions achieve our purposes. In regard to parent-community involvement in schools, we are currently in the situation either where the political principle is in the picture but undiscussed, or dealt with superficially, gingerly, and insincerely, or where power (sometimes naked power) obscures everything else.

In my experience, where power struggle became a central feature, it was not the original purpose of the participants to make power so central but rather in some way to improve the substance and quality of the educational experience. The reasons for the power struggle were many, but the most obvious and common one was the failure or inability or reluctance to begin the discussion with where the participants stood in regard to the political principle. After all, the political principle is not new; it is rooted in our national history and political system; it is one everyone has experienced in his or her life; it is a clear, simple principle (at the same time it is "messy" in implementation). What happened in these

instances was that none of the participants ever discussed the *polit-*
ical principle qua principle but rather became embroiled, almost immediately, in the specifics of power redistribution and the mechanisms
of implementation. I am in no way suggesting that if the discussion
of the principle had taken place, what followed would have been
sweetness and light. What I am suggesting, and I do not think I am
being overly or unrealistically optimistic, is that such a discussion
would have gotten more agreement about the principle than the
open warfare indicated. If such agreement could have been reached,
it could have served as a preventive, in part at least, for a hostile
"we win, you lose" atmosphere. Instead, what happened is that the
professionals started with the Custer-like stance of being surrounded
by deadly enemies, and the parent-community groups started with
the stance that the professionals had erected impenetrable, high
walls to keep "outsiders" outside. Both sides proceeded as if no
agreement on anything was possible, and superior power would be
the ultimate arbiter. Of course, matters were not helped any by the
fact that little or nothing was contained in the education of educators in regard to the history, dilemmas, and opportunities of the
political principle. Nor were matters helped any by the fact that the
outsiders were far from clear (I am being charitable) about *why and
in what ways* their possession of power would improve the quality of
education. That is, it does not follow as night follows day that
because power would be differently allocated and used that education would be improved. The political principle is just that: a political principle about who should participate in some way in decisions
vital to his or her welfare. It speaks to governance, not to the core
problems governance seeks to ameliorate. The virtue of clarity
about the political principle is that it requires you to ask, How do
we concretely act on the basis of the principle to alter and improve
an undesirable situation that is extraordinarily complex? But when
a conflict, potential or actual, degenerates into power plays, the limits of the political principle and the complexity of the educational
issues are given short shrift. The political principle is a starting

point. Reaching agreement on it is, in some respects, easier than
deciding how to proceed to diagnose and treat the deficiencies in
the educational process. In the instances I have observed or read
about (and I have a good counterintelligence network) the substance and contexts of the educational experience remained where
they initially were: on an unlit back burner.

In this chapter I have discussed the obstacles professionals in
general and educators in particular have in enunciating, confronting, and accepting the political principle. If only because parents know and have more contact with teachers than with other
personnel, it is not surprising that when parents are critical of
schools, they have teachers in mind. Someone once said that the
cold war (before the Soviet Union dissolved) really started with
the cold war between teachers and parents, a war that, far from
remaining cold, shows signs of heating up. Teachers, of course, did
not greet that remark warmly. But there is one group of teachers
among whom there are more than a few who, albeit reluctantly,
saw truth in that quip. I refer to teachers whose sons or daughters
(or both) were in a public school and, therefore, as parents met
with the teachers of their children. It was not infrequent in my
experience over the decades to hear these parents criticize teachers
for treating them "as if I was just a parent whose opinions were to
be politely heard but not taken seriously." I cannot, of course, say
that these parent-teachers responded more or less sensitively to the
parents of the children in their classroom. But I bring this up to
emphasize how one's own experiences as an "outsider" can and
should be used to understand how the boundaries of professionalism work against recognition of the political principle. But that
lack of recognition is by no means unusual *within* the profession
(i.e., between those within the same profession but differing in status, function, or responsibility). As I shall discuss in the next chapter, however insensitive teachers may be to the political principle
in regard to parents, they are acutely aware of the principle in their
relationships with those administratively above them; and in turn

each layer of the educational hierarchy is no less aware of the principle in their interaction with the layers above them. Awareness of the principle—more specifically, violations of the principle—depends apparently on whose ox is gored.

If, as I have said, it is understandable that parent-community advocates for taking the political principle seriously primarily have teachers in mind, that focus betrays an ignorance of how power is allocated, experienced, and protected *within* the educational hierarchy of a school and school system. We are used to thinking that as one goes up the layers of the hierarchy (in any complex organization) there is an increasing correlation between status and responsibility, on the one hand, and the exercise of power, on the other hand. That correlation is far smaller than people realize. So, for example, we unreflectively assume that a school principal has and exercises more power than a classroom teacher. And when we make that assumption we mean that the principal, more than the classroom teacher, determines the educational policy of that school, or can alter an existing one. And by educational policy I do *not* refer to making up bus schedules, arranging for supervision of the cafeteria, getting substitute teachers, arranging field trips, or insuring that report cards are handed in on time and in some way conveyed to parents, and so forth. By educational policy I mean such things as how new teachers are to be selected; establishing criteria for and observing teacher effectiveness and classroom climate; how disciplinary problems are to be handled; the obtaining and allocating of existing or new educational materials; providing intellectual-educational stimulation to teachers; serving as spokesperson for the school in discussions of budget; conducting "foreign relations" with higher administrative personnel, parents, and the surrounding community; and more. In matters like these the principal, as the title indicates, is seen as having more power than teachers. The domain of the teacher is the encapsulated classroom, a domain directly or indirectly subject to policies of the principal. A teacher is "just" that: low person on the totem pole of power. As one would expect, it has long been the case that, as a group, teachers have resented being subject to educational policies in the formulation of which they have had no role. Indeed, the rise of militant teacher unions is understandable only if one comprehends the substance of that resentment (which was directed only in part to principals); that is, in their self-interest teachers began to take seriously the political principle. If they were to be affected by policies, they wanted a role in their formulation. It is not happenstance that they began to take the political principle seriously at about the same time that the call for parent-community involvement in educational policy began to be articulated, *although neither of these groups perceived their kinship in regard to the political principle, then or now*. Phenomenologically, teachers are themselves in relation to their administrative superiors precisely the way parent-community groups see themselves in relation to school personnel: outsiders looking and wanting "in." One can only hope that some day these two "outsiders" will better understand their kinship in principle: what is sauce for the goose *is* sauce for the gander. I am, I suppose, indulging the hope that that understanding will lead to an acceptance of the political principle, an acceptance that could prevent the worst excesses of the resort to displays of naked power.

But what about the principal? How does he or she view the power of the position? I have discussed this question with scores of principals, and their answers can be put into three categories, overlapping and cumulative as sources of frustration, as restrictions on the exercise of power. The first category contains the perception that teachers look kindly on a principal who leaves them alone to do what they have always done and/or accedes to requests for this or that; they do not take kindly to suggestions that require the teacher to change what and how he or she teaches, how a class should be organized, how a particular child or type of child should be managed, or to explain why children are performing below standard and to come up with an approach that will improve performance, or to explain why previous suggestions have not been followed. The second category has to do with the "union contract," *a document about which the principal had no role whatsoever* but that contains sentences, phrases, and clauses that either constrict the scope of his or her power or inhibit its exercise because it may result in a grievance procedure, which may make a bad situation worse. As one woman said to me shortly after she became principal of a troubled and troublesome school, "If I did what I know I should do, and what on the level of rhetoric I am expected to do, I would have time for little else other than engaging in grievance procedures, and I would have to defend that to those above me who, despite what they say and expect, would not like it."

The third category is the most poignant: the realization by principals that they must follow and implement educational policies legislated by those higher up in the hierarchy, policies in the formulation of which they played little or no role, and usually no role. I say poignant because those who seek to become principals usually have a vision of what an ideal school should be. They do not seek to be principals to implement the vision of others. So, when they become a principal and begin to experience the culture of the school from that position, it is almost always sobering and frequently disillusioning. As teachers they understood, they experienced, what violations of the political principle meant. As principals they did not expect that again they would be outsiders looking in. It is that kind of experience or reaction that makes it difficult for principals sincerely and seriously to act on the basis of the political principle in their relations with teachers or parent-community groups, actions they perceive as a further dilution of their power.

We are used to hearing that the presidency of the United States is the most powerful position in the world. Few, if any, presidents would agree with that statement on the basis of their experience with the House of Representatives, the Senate, the Supreme Court, their political party and that of the opposition, let alone countless special interest groups. Formally and informally, the presidency is subject to all kinds of restrictions on the explicit powers of the office. Our most effective presidents have had several characteristics. They quickly learned the difference between having power and being influential. To the extent that they were influential it was because they took the political principle seriously; that is, they sought to work with and influence those who had some kind of stake in regard to a proposed policy. They made the boundaries between themselves and diverse stakeholders permeable; they respected (even expected) that those who would be affected by a policy would want some kind of input in the final shape of that policy. And, needless to say, "those" includes the "outsiders," the non-professionals, the people who vote and whom the political system is intended to serve.

What I have said about some presidents can (and should) be said about some schools. Although they are admittedly few, I have known schools (*not* school systems) where the political principle informs relationships among school personnel and between them and parent-community individuals. But in every case respect for the principle was not a matter of formal policy of the school *system* but rather of an unusual and refreshing array of people for whom the principle was, so to speak, second nature. They did not formally proclaim the principle or even put it into words. I cannot put it any other way than to say that they were the kinds of people whose lives seemed to be based on the principle. I put it that way because in some instances the appointment of a new principal and the hiring of one or two new teachers created severe problems because the rhetoric of these new arrivals turned out to be just that: rhetoric devoid of consistency with action. I am certain that there are readers of this book who will have experienced what can happen when new arrivals, especially when they are principals, have little respect for the political principle. The fan can blow other than air!

I have discussed the political principle in the case of teachers and principals. But there are other layers of administrative power above them. Indeed, in our urban school systems, the hierarchy can be quite complex to the point where it is next to impossible to determine who has the power to do what. The lines of power may seem clear on an administrative chart, but the chart has little to do with the realities. Whatever I have said about the sources of disillusionment of principals is true for those "above" them even though most of them had been principals and could have known that the grass is not predictably greener elsewhere. Hope does spring eternal.

In brief, it is an egregious instance of missing the trees for the forest to see the call for parent-community involvement in decision making as a new or challenging expression of the political principle, or to see the resistance of educators to that expression as sheer perversity, or narrowmindedness, or solely as rampant professional imperialism. *Leaving parent-community advocates aside, resistance to the political principle characterizes relationships among the different layers of administrative power in the school system.* The parent-community advocates are latecomers to the scene.

There is one piece of federal legislation that is relevant here because it signaled the third revolution in American education. The first revolution was compulsory education; the second was the 1954 Supreme Court desegregation decision; the third was the 1975 Education for Handicapped Children Act, which required all schools to eliminate the practice of automatically segregating children with disabilities away from "regular" classrooms, practices that had produced two schools within one school building. Contained in that 1975 legislation was what an individual who helped draft it termed "the civil rights section." That section spells out in detail the rights of parents to participate in any forum where decisions about placement of and programs for their child were to be made. Indeed, parents had to approve placement and programs, and in the event they did not they had the right to appeal to special authorities in the state department of education. As the individual who helped draft that section said to me (paraphrased), "We were going to make damned sure that school personnel were no longer going to ignore parents, to act unilaterally without the involvement and approval of parents." As someone who has spent years in and around the special education arena—and participated in federally sponsored meetings intended to examine what the problems of implementation of the new legislation might be—I was less than optimistic about the road ahead. For one thing, it was not legislation most educators had sought or supported. Also, it immediately became obvious, especially in our urban school systems, that the actions consistent with the spirit (and frequently with the letter) of the civil rights section would be rare. Dr. Michael Klaber and I had occasion to review the research literature relevant to the implementation of the civil rights section (Sarason and Klaber, 1985). We were unable, to indulge understatement, to come to encouraging conclusions, and reviews of the literature by others since 1985 came to similar conclusions. I do not report this to scapegoat school personnel because, as is all too frequent, that legislation contained absolutely nothing that recognized what the *predictable* problems would be and the steps that should be taken and supported to prevent, to a discernible degree at least, those predictable problems. It was one thing to mandate practices; it was quite another thing to recognize what was going to happen when the culture of every school in the country was going to be altered in ways strange to its members.

But the main reason I bring up the 1975 legislation is briefly to examine this question: How did that legislation come about? It is a long story, and one of its most important chapters begins in the early 1950s when a small group of parents met and created the National Association for Retarded Children (NARC). And their goal was to exert pressure to provide more and better resources for their children in the public schools where those children were well below first-class citizens, if they were accepted, as many were not, in schools. For these parents schools were seen as immorally insensitive to the educational needs of their children. In those days the parents were not clamoring for "mainstreaming" or "inclusion" but for more and better programs. The NARC soon became one of the most influential, effective lobbying groups in the corridors of political power (local, state, national). Nothing more clearly signifies the change in the substance of the parental stance than in the change of organization's name: The National Association of Retarded Citizens. Citizens have *rights*, not the least of which is encapsulated in what I have called the political principle. And it was the NARC who played a crucial role in embodying the political principle in the civil rights section of the legislation. As someone said, "School people did not know who or what hit them."

It is my opinion that the fate of the parent-community rationale depends on the degree to which the political principle begins to inform relationships within the school system, and there is little evidence that that is beginning to take place. I label that as an opinion. There are those who would argue that on the basis of what has been learned about systems in general and human systems in particular, what I call an opinion is more solid than that. But one thing is clear: taking the political principle seriously in action in one part of a system creates disturbance in other parts of that system. The political principle implies a process—it does not tell us what that process should or could be in particular instances. But before we get to specifics, it is necessary, indeed mandatory, to discuss, as I shall in the next chapter, an implication of the political principle that for all practical purposes has gone undiscussed. It is less an implication than it is a foundation upon which the political principle rests.

Chapter Four

Assets and Deficits

The political principle is one of those "shoulds and oughts" in living that is a basis for judgment and action. When stated simply, as I have done, it all too easy to gloss over, indeed ignore, what is perceived by its advocates as a fact: those seeking participation have knowledge or opinions of some kind vital to the substance of the decision-making process; that is, *they have or are assets*. They do not seek merely to observe that process or to be informed about it but rather to participate *because* they are assets others should know about or use; they represent a vested interest, but that in no way means that what they know is necessarily valid or invalid or irrelevant to a policy or decision. The decision-making process always involves choices among alternative courses of action, judgments of significance of the "facts" for each course and its practical consequences. At its best, the process systematically examines the universe of alternatives to be considered and the weighing of the facts or "data" supporting each alternative. At its worst, it blithely and drastically narrows the universe of alternatives and awareness of available views and data. What the political principle implies is that the decision-making process should reflect the views of all those who will be affected by the ultimate decision. More correctly, it should be a process where those views and their supporting evidence are heard. Those views and evidence may be considered by others as invalid or irrelevant, but that is no warrant for not hearing it if only because what you do not hear may come back to haunt or defeat you.

The crucial point is that those who seek participation see themselves as assets in the decision-making process. Where in "real life" the problem begins is the inability, or reluctance, or refusal to regard those whose views are different than yours, or who have a different status than you do, or whose relevant experience you deem nonexistent, as a justification for giving them a role in the decision-making process. You do not see them as having assets, and, therefore, their participation will muddy the waters, prolong the process, and increase the level of controversy. That stance does not derive only from considerations of power; there is more to it than that, and the "more" is that these people are seen as having nothing to contribute in the way of ideas or knowledge or experience. The questions that arise here are crucial ones: How do we define people as assets? How do we decide that a person has something to contribute? What prevents us from seeing the assets of a person? Let me discuss these questions by several examples.

The first example concerns a child we are told is mentally retarded, or a slow learner, or has a learning disability. Those labels conjure up imagery and characteristics we have assimilated from diverse sources. We have never seen that child, but once we hear the label we have a "picture" of what that child may look like, or experiences, or feels, or acts, or how that child responds to challenges by others. (We may also feel sorry for that child's parents and teachers.) In short, the label is a kind of key opening doors to our imagery, our preconceptions. *Although not always the case, the label and the associated characteristics are a litany of deficits, handicaps, pathologies, and any hint that the individual has assets is notable by its absence.* That use of labels is especially frequent among those in the clinical professions (among which I include teachers and other educators because they are confronted with problem children whom they are required to label, to put into a category). Someone once said that the occupational disease of those in these professions is that they cannot recognize an asset in an individual because they are schooled to apply labels denoting deficits. Someone else put it this way: clinicians cannot recognize an asset unless hit over the head with disconfirming evidence. Let me illustrate the point with a personal example in which I do not come up smelling like roses.

It was when I was a clinical psychologist in a state training school for mentally retarded individuals. Admission day was Tuesday. Looking out of my office window I saw a car pull up, and from the rear door emerged a man carrying what appeared to be a very large infant-child. My heart sank because no child below the age of six could be admitted. To make a long story short, that small child was a thirty-one-year-old man who was being institutionalized because his mother, who for years had been his sole living parent, had just died. He was also the worst and most gnarled-involved case of cerebral palsy I had (or have) ever seen. His body was in constant motion, he drooled from the mouth, and his head, which seemed to be half of his body, had a face that can best be described as wild. I had two reactions. First, he belonged (and I placed him) in a cottage for very low-functioning individuals. He merited the label "very retarded." Second, there was obviously no reason to formally evaluate him within three days, as was our custom (i.e., I knew what a formal evaluation would contain). Well, a week or so later I was walking past his cottage, and I met Mr. Rooney, the house father. "How is the Humphrey boy doing?" I asked. To which Mr. Rooney replied, "He is one smart cookie." So, consistent with the dynamics of the labeling process I said to myself, "Another instance of an untrained person coming to erroneous conclusions." I asked Mr. Rooney to explain. "I can't," he said, "but if you come in I can show you." In I went and there was Mr. Humphrey lying on the seat of the wheelchair as if it were a cradle. Mr. Rooney left for a moment and came back with a checkerboard (which had accompanied Mr. Humphrey on admission!), the spaces on which serially contained the letters of the alphabet. "Now," Mr. Rooney said, "ask him a question that requires a one-word answer. Move your finger slowly along the alphabet. Although he is always in motion, when he wants you to stop at a letter he will *really* go into motion." My first question was, "Who is president of the United States?" And following Mr. Rooney's instruction, this "low-grade" individual spelled *Roosevelt (FDR)*. Let us not be detained by descriptions of my chagrin and temporary humbleness. (I have a collection of such personal cases that I used with graduate clinical psychology students in my course Humbleness 101.) The significance of the case is how it illustrates two completely different stances. *I saw deficits. His mother had seen deficits and assets, and she capitalized on the assets.* I was the all-knowing professional; she was "only" a parent.

A second example is Wayne Adams, a fifth-grade black who was performing on a third-grade level in a ghetto school. Put most succinctly, Wayne was a grand pain in the neck to the teacher. It was hard for her to get and sustain his attention, he frequently roamed the room, and he rarely finished assignments the teacher specially designed for him to do at his desk. My role in that school was to accept referrals from teachers about problem children, visit the classroom to observe the referred child, and then confer with the teacher about management and disposition issues. In Wayne's case the teacher presented me with a list of his inadequacies, ending with the plea that he be removed from her class. I observed him for almost two hours and, with one exception, saw what the teacher had observed. The one exception was that I noticed that every now and then he would turn over the assignment sheet, and for a period of minutes he would studiously be drawing something with his pencil. I would walk to his desk, watch him draw, and I would express my delight, and it was sincere delight, at his facility in making pictures. I got some colored pencils and large papers and asked him if he wanted to use them. He smiled broadly and for the next half hour absorbed himself in drawing a variety of pictures; the fluidity of his movements, his use of contrasting colors, and the impression conveyed by each of the several drawings were striking. When I discussed this with the teacher, she said she knew about his drawings, but to her that illustrated how unable Wayne was to direct attention to his assignment. To her the activity was a deficit; to me it was an asset that could be utilized. That the boy was academically retarded was obvious; that he possessed an abiding interest and talent could not be recognized or utilized by the teacher.

A third example was a young woman who had been diagnosed as mentally retarded, came from a horrendous family background, and was institutionalized at age fifteen. She was a quiet, shy person whom everybody liked. At the same time she was regarded as fit for only very menial tasks (e.g., washing floors, working in the laundry). In short, she was without assets, aside from being likeable. Several years after commitment she was assigned to the hospital laboratory to do the simplest of routine tasks. One year later she was able to perform the following tasks:

1. Sterilization and chemical cleansing of glassware used in bacteriology and quantitative chemistry

2. Preparation of bacterial media, physiological and chemical solutions used in bacteriology, hematology, and qualitative chemistry

3. Cleansing of volumetric, graduated, and hematological pipettes and special chemical filters

4. Complete urinalysis, except for microscopic including qualitative and quantitative sugars, albumin, acetone tests, and specific gravity

5. Streaking and plating of bacterial cultures with aseptic technique

6. Assistance in quantitative blood and tissue chemistry as in total proteins, lipids, sodiums, and potassiums

7. Staining of hematology and bacterial slides

8. Taking stool cultures and finger blood tests alone

9. Keeping daily record of work performed

10. All blood typing (All work was, of course, checked by the head of the laboratory.)

By year's end she was receiving and responding to instruction in the use of the microscope. How to begin to explain the discovery of "assets," which no one would have predicted? What the reader needs to know is that the head of the laboratory was a woman who, as a result of polio, had no use of her legs, used crutches, and had great difficulty going from one part of the lab to another. What is crucial is that a loving child-parent relationship quickly developed, as a result of which the head of the lab found herself *believing* that the girl was capable of more than her case history and psychological test results indicated. I italicize *believing* to emphasize that, as the head of the lab told me, "she not only was loveable and wanted so much to be of more help to me, that I decided to 'test' her, to see if she was as potentially capable as I dearly hoped." The head of the lab did not see the young girl through the prisms of her case history and psychological test results, containing as they did the listing and description of inadequacies and deficits. Like Mr. Humphrey's mother, she came to believe that the girl potentially had assets, she *wanted* to believe that, and she put that belief to the test.

One more example, but this time it is about normal, bright college-bound high school seniors. As we shall see, in this example the label "high school students" conjured up imagery and characteristics, perceived deficits, and if not for certain circumstances, there would be no story for me to tell.

A colleague of mine, Dr. Richard Sussman, visited with the professor who had supervised his master's degree work in child development. He met with her and her research assistants to find out on which research problems they were working. They described a number of studies they wished to carry out, but, he was told, they faced two seemingly insuperable obstacles: they needed several elementary school populations, and the schools they had approached either were reluctant to cooperate or simply said no. Dr. Sussman then said (condensed and paraphrased), "I could make available to you the number of schools you need if you would agree to the following: I would select eight to ten high school seniors whom you would train to collect your data, and you would give them a miniseminar on data analysis." The response of the researchers was predictable: "How can we entrust high school seniors to collect research data from children? Granted that you would select bright, motivated youngsters, but, after all, they are high school students who have never participated in research, their interpersonal skills and judgment are far from fully formed, they are not used to assuming serious responsibilities, and is it not realistic to expect that they will make mistakes and blunders contaminating the data and perhaps resulting in the school stopping the research? Then where will we be?" Whatever the characteristics the label "high school seniors" connoted and denoted to the researchers, it included several they considered deficits in regard to their pursuits. That is to say, the label referred to positive and negative characteristics and imagery. But the researchers were understandably desperate; they had studies ready to go and no place to carry them out. They agreed to Dr. Sussman's proposal. The studies were carried out with exemplary speed and quality. The researchers were so impressed and grateful that they invited the students to give a colloquium at the university; they also gave a presentation to their board of education.

Labeling is a normal, useful human cognitive attribute. To be opposed to labeling is like being opposed to breathing. Like so many other attributes it can have untoward uses and consequences. Nowhere is this more clear than when we use labels in ways that divert our attention to peoples' deficits, downplaying or even totally ignoring their assets. That person is a black therefore . . . That person is a woman therefore . . . That person is old therefore . . . That person is on welfare therefore . . . That person is a socialist therefore . . . How many times are these labels used to refer to deficits, inadequacies, inferiorities, and other undesirable attributes?

All of the above is prologue to the attempt to answer the question: *Leaving considerations of power aside*, what are the assets, actual or potential, of people we label as parents? Far too many teachers use the label "parent" frequently as a putdown, especially in these days when parents and others seek a role in educational decision making. That is why I ask the reader to try, as I shall try, to define the assets of parents as well as their deficits in regard to matters educational. That, I should hasten to say, does not mean that these are assets all parents have or that the deficits are characteristics of all parents. Indeed, that is the major point: we must avoid using the label as if all those on whom we pin it are homogeneous, which obviously they are not.

1. Parents have knowledge of their child not available to anyone else (i.e., knowledge about learning style, interests, motivation, problems, and talents). That knowledge, regardless of how others may regard its degree of validity or interpretive significances, is and should be usable by those who are responsible for that child's formal education. Parents want that knowledge to be usable by others; they see that knowledge as an asset to be mined.

2. Parents have, to indulge understatement, a serious interest in the formal education experiences of their child. They are not indifferent to how their child is faring. They want to be informed and consulted, they want to be helpful, they do not want to be passive. If they want to be informed, they also want to inform. If they are not indifferent to being informed, they do not want others to be indifferent to what they think they know. Interest has at least two consequences: appreciation for help that is offered, and appreciation of the opportunity to be helpful.

3. Parents *are* teachers (i.e., educators), and it is inevitable that they come to conclusions about what is good or bad teaching. If those conclusions derive from the family context (a type of classroom), those conclusions are generalized to the school classroom. That kind of generalization cannot be ignored or summarily rejected. It may or may not be valid; it has to be discussed and judged, not thrown out of court, so to speak, because of its origins. Those kinds of conclusions and generalizations are potential assets, not "noise" in the forums of discussion. It is an asset, not a deficit,

that parents do come to conclusions about what teaching is and should be, just as it is an asset when an ill person exercises independent judgment to conclude that he or she is receiving proper or improper medical care.

4. In their role as citizens, parents are accountable for what schools are in the sense that they (and others) provide the monies making school possible. But accountability, again inevitably, involves more than money and that more is contained in the saying that a community gets the kinds of schools it is willing to pay for; that is, the word *willing* implies that citizens have arrived at conclusions about what schools are or should be. It is an asset that parents do not see themselves as only passive taxpayers but as people capable of coming to conclusions about what schools are or should be. You may not agree with those conclusions (they may send you up a wall), but that should not prevent you from recognizing that parents have given you information it is in your interests to know and deal with.

5. By virtue of special interests, hobbies, vocation, and community role, any group of parents has members who possess knowledge and skills that can be used in the education of students and can be a source of stimulation to teachers. More than that, not infrequently these are knowledge and skills many schools could not afford to purchase. Educators tend to define an asset or resource as that which you pay for and, therefore, control; if they cannot purchase it, they cannot have it. If I have learned anything over the years, it is that many parents (and others in the community) are willing to give their expertise if it furthers the intellectual-educational development of students. If many actors want to play Hamlet, there are many parents who would seize the opportunity to be with and teach students *if that opportunity is recognition of their special knowledge and skills that they can convey and demonstrate in their own ways*. I am reminded here of the physician-parent, a professor of anesthesiology, who for an hour on three successive mornings discussed and demonstrated (using film and lab animals) the rationale for and differential consequences of using the most frequently used anesthetics. I

observed on the third day. When the parent left, the students agreed that those sessions were indeed memorable and curiosity satisfying and arousing. The teacher told me that what he had seen and learned would affect his teaching in diverse ways.[1]

My list of assets is not exhaustive, but it is sufficient as a basis for making three points *independent of power considerations or customary professional prerogatives*. I italicize those words because nothing blinds you more effectively to perceiving and utilizing the assets of others than to view them in terms of labels and power status, a view most efficiently inculcated in us in our professional training and even more efficiently reinforced by the hierarchical structure of school systems. As I can attest from my own professional training and experience, unimprisoning yourself from the fetters of professional preciousness is extraordinarily difficult, especially when those fetters seem so natural, right, and proper. I am not being antiprofessional, which would be stupidly mindless. I am saying that professionalism is a mixed blessing, and to deny that is to believe that our view of ourselves as a person and professional is grounded only in cold reason and objective fact. Would that it were so!

The point of the list of assets is that an asset is not only in the

---

[1] This is an infrequent but by no means rare instance of a school capitalizing on the knowledge and skills of parents and others in the community. However, in the instances I have observed or have knowledge about, the schools did not, as a matter of course or procedure, systematically determine which parents and others had skills and knowledge relevant, applicable, and available to the substance and goals of the curriculum. That is to say, in modern jargon they did not have or seek that kind of "database." I am quite aware that using such a database confronts problems of time, logistics, administration, *and* educational policy. But if and how those problems should be confronted and decided are *not* issues to be resolved in forums of which parents and others have no role, assets go unused.

The most inspiring and instructive example I know is what Kenneth Koch, a well-known poet, did in getting children in an elementary, New York ghetto school to write poetry! He describes why, what, and how he accomplished his goals in a fascinating book, *Wishes, Lies, and Dreams* (1970).

eye of the beholder but that the definition of that asset does and should change as a result of changing needs or circumstances, imagination and creativity, and courage. There was a time when oil was "just" oil, a lubricant for the moving parts of machinery, for example, automobiles. It did not take long before oil became a basis for a huge petrochemical industry productive of a literally fantastic array of products. Oil was not "just" oil—it became a very differentiated asset. Similarly, parents (and others) are not just parents; they have assets, actual and potential, applicable to the formal education of their children. If their assets have been narrowly seen and defined, it has been because circumstances were no challenge to such a view, there was no need to change that view, and there was no political-moral basis to initiate the redefinition process. Educators have always complained that resources made available to them were limited. Resources are always limited. Their complaint was always accompanied by requests for increased budgets to hire more personnel and purchase more and better materials. I would be the last to assert that those complaints were always without any merit. However, their awareness of limited resources did not cause them to redefine parents and others as differentiated, usable assets. But in our social world and the arena of education many changes have taken place and new needs and issues have arisen in the post–World War II era, with unsettling consequences for school personnel. The first had to do with the seriousness with which the political principle began to be articulated. The second had to do with the public's dissatisfactions with the quality and outcomes of schooling. The third, and most germane to this chapter, is the conclusion that the correlation between increasing budgets and educational outcomes is not much, if at all, above zero. That conclusion is one that many school personnel reluctantly (but privately) are expressing.

School personnel do not deny that schools are not accomplishing agreed-upon goals. And on the level of rhetoric (i.e., public pronouncements) school personnel accept the political principle when it is stated vaguely. Let us not gloss over the fact that in almost all instances where the political principle has been institutionalized, it has not been because school personnel had been its advocate but rather because it was mandated-legislated by others. Despite these changing circumstances there has been no serious, searching discussion of parents and others as differentiated assets, as a kind of "venture capital" that could be profitable to schools. I use the words *venture capital* advisedly (and metaphorically) because they refer to "investments" that give promise of being profitable, but there is risk that they may not be. I shall discuss this in greater detail in a later chapter.

Before turning to the deficits of parents and others, it is important—it is also obvious—to say that the assets of parents cannot be perceived and realized by educators unless the relationship between the two parties bears the stamp of respect and trust. And when those features are absent you have the situation where people talk, if they talk at all, past and not with each other.

In a paper entitled "Total Quality for Americans" Elizabeth Holmes (1993) succinctly and incisively (and remarkably) compares and contrasts Japanese and American culture in regard to institutionalizing total quality management (TQM) in business and industrial settings. What she has to say in the following excerpt is no less appropriate to the educational arena where the political principle is a central issue.

> Individuality, of course, has traditionally played a strong, if somewhat limited, role in American business. In a command and control environment, it is a few individuals who call the shots. The rest are rewarded and recognized, individually, for how well they carry out the orders. In this environment, leadership has been defined as a set of traits that an individual in command either has or doesn't have.
>
> To make it work for TQM, however, we must shift our emphasis on it away from the person in authority to all the contributors to quality processes. In particular, given the central role of teamwork in TQM, we must develop a new understanding of how individuality can play out in teams and team leadership.

We can begin to do this by emphasizing that individuality is not lost in a team. A team may be understood as a group of diverse individuals, each contributing something necessary to what the group is trying to achieve. And we can point out that leadership need not be vested in one person but leadership roles can be played by a variety of people as the situation and individual expertise dictate. In order for this to be workable, of course, we must see that each team member is prepared to assume a leadership role if necessary. This is not an easy task, given the leadership roles that a team typically requires (for instance, supervising, teaching, coaching, mentoring, consulting, and mediating), but each role can be learned, practiced, measured, and improved over time.

There is another issue related to making individuality work for TQM: Historically, individuality has often been stifled in our organizations. Even now, organizations that apparently invite individual contributions may unconsciously thwart them by sending out strong, but silent, messages that only certain topics are discussible. I have talked with many people, whose organizations purport to have robust and effective quality processes, who have expressed serious doubts about their ability to raise process questions with their bosses. These people, who are themselves in very high positions, feel that such questions may be seen as challenges to the authority, or even the intelligence, of their bosses. By this unconscious repression we shut down the very power source, our individuality that we need to make our TQM run.

Let us now turn to the deficits of parent-community individuals and groups in regard to participation. As we shall see deficits are not of a piece, nor are they irremediable.

1. Parents have little basis for understanding the culture of a school and school system: the axioms and assumptions undergirding behavioral and programmatic regularities; the nature and rationale for decision making in regard to scores of problems and responsibilities; how organizational-educational goals and practices

are experienced and interpreted by *adults* in that culture, varying as they do with status, power, and experience; and how within that culture, and between it and the "outside," are attitudes or stances the origins and substance of which are rooted in a present and past. A school or school system is a complicated affair that did not have a virginal birth and is not easily described or comprehended. Nor is it a static affair devoid of tensions, conflicts, and doubts about goals, practices, and outcomes. If most people know (or think they know) more about how and why the federal government operates with varying degrees of effectiveness, than it does about a school or school system, it is because there are media whose job it is to inform the public about this or that aspect of government policy, action, and effectiveness.

2. Parents' knowledge of and attitudes toward schooling in general and school personnel in particular derive primarily from their experience as students. That is both an asset and a deficit, an experiential asset not to be ignored but at the same time a deficit because that type of experience gives rise to attitudes about classrooms, teachers, and subject matter that are narrow in perspective, that cannot be understood in terms of the perspectives from which school personnel perceive students, classroom practices, subject matter, educational goals, and more. Just as children and their parents comprehend "family life" very differently, schoolchildren and school personnel comprehend schooling very differently. *That does not mean that the comprehension by parents and school personnel is necessarily adequate or valid but that their "pictures" are different; that is, they are differences that make a difference in the real world of action and relationships.*

3. When parents and others call for involvement of some degree or kind in the decision-making process, their emphasis is on issues of power—they want "in"—and not on substantive educational issues (e.g., what life in a classroom should be, the classroom contexts for productive learning, the pros and cons for the use of tests and test scores, how one becomes aware of alternative con-

ceptions of curriculum, how resources outside of the school can be made available to buttress and expand the substance and effectiveness of classroom learning). To seek power is to raise and begin to answer the question: to seek power to change, *what?* Changing the forces of power in no way guarantees that anything else will change. To seek power in order to become more knowledgeable, which does not mean becoming an expert, requires confronting your assets and deficits. To seek power without asking the "what" question is not only to beg the question but to avoid it and, therefore, to collude in cosmetic changes.

There are those who will conclude that these deficits are reasons enough to resist involvement by parents and others. That conclusion is justified if you make several assumptions. The first is that the political principle is inappropriate in this instance, or that it is appropriate only in very narrow confines (i.e., educational issues are off-limits). The second assumption is that the assets of parents are not assets. That is to say, they are not assets relevant to educational issues. The third is that the deficits are not remediable, in part at least; parents cannot become more knowledgeable to the point where they have something to contribute to changing and improving the quality of schooling, perhaps to bring new life, new blood to an educational arena about which few within and without it are satisfied. The fourth assumption is "this too shall pass"; that is, the issue, like a lot of fads and fashions, will run its course. I have heard that said by more than a few educators at the same time they bemoan the fecklessness of many schools, and some, in fact, see the situation getting worse.

If I do not agree with any of these assumptions, it is not because I consider parent involvement a proved means for improving schools but because my adherence to the political principle requires it, and there is every reason to believe that the issue will not go away. When the political principle will be taken seriously and sincerely (hope springs eternal, I know), it will take educators off the hook of being *solely* responsible and accountable for the plight of our school. At the present time, educators feel like General Custer surrounded by enemies, with no supportive constituencies, and dependent only on hope for a secular miracle. But there can be a supportive constituency, a participating one possessed of assets and remediable deficits, a constituency that at the very least will seek to prevent efforts (mindless for the most part) to bypass, or weaken, or even dismantle the public schools. Those efforts will gain force to the extent that the public's criteria for judging schools continue not to be met. That, in fact, is what I have predicted (orally and in print) over the last thirty-five years, and candor requires that I say I now believe the situation will get worse. More about this later in this book.

Whatever I have listed and said about the assets and deficits of parents is in principle precisely what educational administrators have said about the role of teachers in educational decision making. When I articulated this kinship to groups of teachers, there were several reactions. The first was a mixture of silence, reflection, and then consternation. The second was (paraphrase) "The analogy does not wash. Community people do not know schools; they have little basis, if any, for understanding why a teacher does what she does, or even a quarter of the things that goes in a school. As teachers we know schools. No one can deny that, not even administrators." To which I would reply, "I do deny it. I think it is a fact that over the decades I have known and talked with more administrators, usually principals, than anyone in this room. Given my age, it may well be that the number I have talked with exceeds the combined number of all administrators under whom all in this group have worked. If there is anything about which they agreed it is that the individual teacher does not know all that goes on in a school. Indeed, they would say, each teacher sees the school in terms of *her* thinking, practices, problems, and biases and, therefore, does not comprehend why things cannot be otherwise. Teachers are *individualists* in terms of their space and psychology; they do not know, and often they are not interested in, how a *whole* school works and why. We thank God when a teacher does her job in the classroom well but that does not mean that because she does her job well she understands the larger picture and can contribute to it."

I would sometimes bring up a personal example relevant to the above. It was when I was director of a psychoeducational clinic at Yale. I was sitting in my office trying to understand why I was having difficulty with my department in regard to obtaining additional resources. "Suddenly" the clouds parted and the sun shed its light. You have, I said to myself, to ask two questions. Who tries to "make it" in the university? Whom does the university select? The two questions had one answer: *rugged individualism*. Put briefly, by virtue of factors of selection and self-selection the university guarantees that it will be comprised of bright, ambitious, prima donna types who do not seek or know how to work with each other and frequently do not know how to talk with each other. And each sees the university in idiosyncratic, self-serving ways (of which I was a fairly good example). I began to understand why university administrators see faculty as lovable, demanding, pouting children who confused *their* world with the world of the university. And that is what educational administrators were conveying to me about teachers. The irony is that university and school administrators are victims of the self-fulfilling prophecy: they pin their labels on the faculty and then act in ways that prove to them that the labels are appropriate (i.e., the "deficits" of the faculty are irremediable). If that is not nonsense, it comes close to it. I am *not* suggesting that the problem has a "solution" in the sense that four divided by two is a solution. In the realm of human-organizational relationships we rarely, if ever, deal with problems that have once-and-for-all solutions. But if those kinds of problems have no final solutions, it does not mean they cannot be ameliorated.

In regard to parental involvement the major obstacle at present is that the relationships between the two sides center around power and turf, a situation conducive to nonproductive struggle. Some would argue that altering power relationships never occurs without struggle. More specifically, that the ideology of professionalism is so strong, so concerned with boundaries of authority and responsibility, as to make alterations in power anathema to professionals, and educators are by no means unusual in that respect. But we are discussing educators and cannot ignore the fact that a good fraction of the general public perceives educators as unable and unwilling to agree to changing power relationships, and, as I have emphasized, that is also true for relationships between teachers and their professional "higher ups."

I shall return to this problem in later chapters. Let us in the next chapter turn to some "facts of life" that confirm the adage "problem creation through problem solution." That is, once you accept the political principle, "messiness" escalates, which is why so many professionals and their leaders prefer a more directive-authoritarian style of organization in which "things get done" *efficiently*, even though that style may in practice be self-defeating of organizational goals.

Chapter Five

From Theory to Practice

There are two related immediate consequences of taking the political principle seriously. The first is that you enlarge the range of points of view and of vested interests given expression in the process of educational decision making. That is usually experienced as a mixed blessing, even by those who advocated and fought for the principle. On the one hand, you take satisfaction from being consistent with the principle; on the other hand, enlargement always (certainly *almost* always) means competing points of view that, if only because of the rules of courtesy, cannot be summarily dismissed, let alone ignored. Even when the decision-making process has not been enlarged to represent "outsiders," you expect that there will be competing points of view (except, of course, when there is that degree of authoritarian leadership as to make the expression of competing points of view dangerous and to make silence the handmaiden of survival, a too-frequent state of affairs).

The decision-making process is not only a forum for competing points of view but one in which they are challenged, their empirical basis flushed out and examined, points of agreement and disagreement clarified and sharpened, and a final decision made according to previously agreed rules. The decision-making process is not a charade, a going through the motions, a process the outcome of which has been predetermined, an occasion in which one's obligation is only to vote shortly after the meeting has been convened. Participants may be unequal in status, knowledge, and power—and it is usually the case that they see each other in those terms—but if they are part of the process, it is because they represent a point of view they are obligated to state and defend. But, again leaving "outsiders" outside, there is a feature of the process that "insiders" tend not to articulate: those with competing points of view seek to provide information and evidence to each other that will persuade others to alter their views, and in so seeking to persuade, they assume others are "remediable" (i.e., with the information and evidence you provide, they will alter their point of view).

I am, of course, describing the process in ideal terms, as if all participants are coolly rational and predisposed to listen to others, *hear* them, reflect on what they say, and to be sufficiently secure so as not to be unduly resistant to changing their point of view. *Yes, it is an ideal description, but does it require special defense to say that we should judge ourselves and others should judge us, by how near we approach or how far we depart from the ideal?* Are participants there to learn, to help others learn, or are they there because they have cornered the market on evidence and truth and cannot distinguish between tunnel vision and a new horizon, or that they have a monopoly on truth that renders the "marketplace of ideas" unnecessary? It is these kinds of considerations that were the basis of my assertion in the previous chapter that it was unjustified for educators to regard the deficits of parent-community advocates as "irremediable." It is deserving of reiteration to say that even when those advocates are not represented, each of the different layers in the educational hierarchy view those below them as irremediable in terms of what they understand and have to contribute to the decision-making process.

A personal example. I retired from Yale in 1989. With one exception, there are few things I miss in not being an active member of my department. The exception was the meetings of the full professors where fateful decisions were made. For a department there is no more important decision than adding a new member, from the inside or outside. I always came to those meetings (having read and reflected on all available materials) secure in how I was going to vote. Often the decision was about an individual in an area other than mine. Nevertheless, I came with a decision I was prepared to defend and, not being a shrinking violet, my explanation for my decision would be civil, loud, and clear, even though it was in regard to an area in which I was by no means expert. In the forty five years I was at Yale participating in those (and similar) meetings, my best estimate is that in the course of the meetings I changed my decision at least 35 percent of the time. I would listen to the opinions of others, their way of evaluating the individual, their conception of departmental needs, and more. And when I found myself changing my mind it was accompanied by self-castigation: why didn't I think of those points, why was I so smug, how more stupid could I be, is there a pill I could take for increasing humbleness? (I need not go into the dynamics of the need to be right and perfect.) Now, you would think that having learned the lesson the first time I would not have to learn it again. Famous last words! It was a lesson I had to learn again and again, and I learned it, albeit incompletely. But there was one feature of those meetings that must be mentioned: there was trust and respect among the members, which is it not to say they necessarily liked each other, given that each of us was a prima donna. And that meant that even if you were discussing substantive problems in an area in which you had little expertise, you had the right and obligation to express your opinion (i.e., to be listened to, heard, and responded to). I learned more and gave more than in any other departmental forum. I have reason to believe that others regarded my lack of expertise as "remediable" just as I came to regard others in the same way. This is not to suggest that these meetings were easy, smooth, and brief. After all, we were not discussing piddling issues. We were faced with decisions with which the department would have to live for a long time.

So, what will predictably happen when parents and others have some kind of role in educational decision making, keeping in mind that even before their inclusion the decision-making forum or process already contains individuals varying considerably in their expertise, status, power, and inexperience in taking the obligations of the political principle seriously? You have enlarged the range of views, of potential points of controversy, the role of personal style, and the remediable-irremediable problem, far from remaining under the table, will be on the table. In brief, enlargement brings complications in its wake. That is predictable. It may be otherwise in Camelot but not in organizations on this earth. Schools are not unique in this respect, just different.

The other immediate consequence of taking the political principle seriously is *time:* where to find and include it within the confines of the ordinary school day (which includes that occasional hour or so after students have left for the day). Time is the tyrannical phenomenon in schooling. For all practical purposes, the school day is finite, divided into segments each of which has an assigned goal that for most conscientious teachers—and in my experience most teachers are conscientious—is not reached because of a lack of time. Phenomenologically, there is a vast difference between what a teacher does accomplish and what he or she would like to accomplish or is expected to accomplish. We are used to hearing that the aim of schooling is to help *each* child "realize his or her full potential." If there were a Guinness book of records for articulated nonsense, that aim, given the time available in the school day, would be a top entry. The aim is laudatory; the time available to do justice to that aim is nonexistent, which is why teachers, especially new teachers, are plagued with guilt about the discrepancy between their perception of what they see are the needs of individual students and the time available to meet those needs. It is no different in the case of administrators who, in one or another way, say that time is finite, and problems and paperwork are infinite.

There is no time during the day for teachers to talk with each other. I shall never forget the first time I tried to arrange a meeting in the school day between me and four high school teachers. It was literally impossible, given how their schedules were organized. As one of the teachers said, "I don't even have time to pee." How about after school? They reluctantly agreed, but they must have sensed that I would misconstrue their reluctance as a lack of motivation and interest. One of them had the courage to say, "By the end of the day I am *drained,* besides which I spend an hour or so after school reading essays, scoring tests I have given, and figuring out what I will do tomorrow." Those were the days before dual-career marriages were as frequent as they are today, but they were days when male teachers not infrequently had second jobs in an effort to bring to family living a semblance of graciousness. In today's era of dual-career marriages in which marriage partners have different and overlapping family responsibilities, time has become a more precious commodity. It is obvious that when parents and others become part of the decision-making process, still another demand will be made on the allocation of time.

The interaction between the two immediate consequences of parental involvement engenders a host of problems among which three are predictable, troublesome, and potentially self-defeating of the spirit of involvement. The first (about which I will say more in the next chapter) has to do with the kinds of issues the group is empowered by others to discuss and decide, or when an issue has been vaguely defined, it has to be decided by the group. From what I have observed and read, it is usually the case that the definition of the issue has all of the characteristics of an ink blot, characteristics that leave a lot of room for conflict, especially when parental involvement has been preceded by controversy, or it has been mandated by those at the top of the organizational pyramid or by legislative fiat. What I call the "perception of messiness" comes to the fore. Accustomed as most of us are to guidelines in which all i's have been dotted and all t's crossed, ambiguity of stated purposes and procedures is no easy situation with which to have to deal. It not only takes time if only because the number of represented interests has been enlarged, but it can, and usually does, bring to the surface power plays and premature efforts to come to a decision *quickly* "so we can do what we are supposed to do." When time is precious, it is all too easy for the desire for "efficiency" to subvert principle and purpose. If it is understandable, it is not excusable. I am not, of course, an advocate for inefficiency. And I am agonizingly aware that in the "real world" time is limited, a fact of life with which we must deal. But that is no justification for using efficiency as synonymous with accomplished purpose.

The second of the three problems is how *final* decisions are to be made and who will make them. Is it by majority vote? The principal? An elected chairperson? This is not a problem with an obvious, simple answer (e.g., majority vote). It could be argued that where everyone is accountable no one is accountable. It could then be argued that the majority has the right to make, with the best of intentions, the wrong decision but that more often than not the majority will make what turns out to be the right decision, and here one could refer to the fact that although we have elected some inadequate presidents, we have elected many who were adequate and some who were superb. Why, some would counter, do we delegate to a senator or congressman the power to vote for us on the basis that he or she presumably knows what his or her constituency thinks, or how divided they are, and is more knowledgeable about the pros and cons of a particular issue than most of those he or she represents? I think it fair to say that of the three branches of the federal government the Supreme Court is held in the highest esteem. And, yet, the court consists of political appointees, usually with wide experience and legal knowledge, and with life tenure rendering them impervious to pressures from special interest groups with great power. As someone once said, "The Supreme Court can tell the majority of citizens that a legislative act they favored is wrong (i.e., unconstitutional), and if they don't like the court's decision, they can go fly a kite."

These are the kinds of questions that over a period of months occupied the constitutional convention of 1787. The more you will read about that convention the more you will appreciate the wisdom in Mencken's assertion that *for every problem there is a simple answer that is wrong.* And let us remember that the founding fathers included a process for amending the Constitution, which they did not regard as a once-and-for-all-time document written and preserved in concrete and then encased in a social vacuum.

So, in regard to parental involvement how will or should final decisions be made? I confess that I do not have *an* answer, the way four divided by two is two is an answer. I am quite aware that the kind of forum and process we are discussing should be conducted according to agreed-upon rules, regulations, laws—call them what you will. We are, we are told, as a society committed to the rule of law, not of individuals. No quarrel there. But (there is always a but) the implementation of laws or rules *consistent with the spirit of them* depends on, at least, two crucial, bedrock considerations. The first is that we confront the *predictable* consequences of a rule in light of what we know about why the rule was necessary in the first place. Passing laws or formulating rules is one thing, the easy part, relatively speaking. Changing or influencing the hearts of people—their values, prejudices, outlooks, perspectives—is the hard part. We have scores of laws prohibiting racial, religious, gender discrimination— for which I thank God for big favors—but in passing such laws there was no justification whatever for failing to confront and examine the problems that would predictably arise. That does not mean that we can prevent those problems, but it does mean that we can prevent, in part at least, the disillusionment that is a consequence of confusing the letter with the spirit of the law, of downplaying the obstacles inherent in what we know are the social realities and indulging our hopes for and vision of an unclouded future.

The 1954 desegregation decision mightily affected my relationship with friends and colleagues, almost all of whom were ecstatic as if the problem of racial prejudice had been solved, or would be in their (then) young lifetimes. Desegregated schools would be the vehicle for achieving racial understanding and harmony. In no uncertain terms I told them they were nuts. Of course the decision was long overdue, but, again of course, the road ahead would be predictably rough, frequently impassable, at best it would be mammothly frustrating, and it was not unrealistic to say that *maybe* there was no light at the end of the tunnel ahead. The letter of the decision was one thing; realizing its spirit in action was another thing, *given the realities of past and present.* I was seen as a cynic, pessimist, even a nihilist. There are and were times when I so labeled myself because I gave up hope that in regard to social change the "changers" seemed capable of confronting *predictable* problems, adopting time perspectives and rationales for action that, far from *preventing* anything, guaranteed that the need for *repair* would become greater. In regard to parent-community involvement in educational decision making, and based on my own observations and the reports of others (I have a rather wide and effective counterintelligence network), what I have said above is, unfortunately, accurate.[1] (My batting average is far from a thousand, but that is another story.)

There is a second consideration that determines the quality and outcomes of implementation of the spirit of involvement, and here again I shall relate a personal anecdote in order to give concrete meaning to two words that otherwise may sound virtuous and empty.

Several years after the Yale Psycho-Educational Clinic was created, and I was its director, I thought it appropriate that a book be written describing what we had done and learned. It was not a book I could or should write by myself because most of the interesting and important projects at the clinic had been done by at least four other individuals, all of whom were junior to me in faculty status. It is easy to characterize these young men. They were bright (very bright), thinkers and doers (this was in the sixties), creative, pas-

---

[1] There are two exceptions about which I have direct knowledge and experience. One is described in *When a College Collaborates with a School* (Trubowitz and others, 1984). That book describes the first five years of their efforts; they are currently writing up the next ten years. The other project is that now being carried out by Dr. Paul Heckman of the University of Arizona in Tucson, an ongoing study confirmatory of almost every point I have made in these pages. Both projects are refreshing examples of taking the political principle seriously.

sionate, articulate in the extreme, not capable of intellectual and personal intimidation by others, and intent (like me) on saving the world. They were distinctive characters, although if you called them rugged individualists, they would recoil because that label had for them a pejorative connotation. Believe me, they were rugged individualists!

I met with the four of them and presented my suggestions about who should write which chapters. I also said (it was not a suggestion) what the order of authorship would be. No problem whatsoever. They were delighted, eager to get started on a book that would be quite hefty. And then I said the following to them. "There is a predictable problem that derives from what I am and you are. One aspect is that under no conditions will I have my name on a book that does not meet my admittedly personal criteria for good writing and thinking. The other aspect of the predictable problem is that each of you is in no doubt about what you want to say and how you will say it. I know it will not happen often, but there will be times when we will clash—we will disagree. As in our past relationship we will find ourselves arguing, yelling, even shouting, pounding the table and other features that have made life at the clinic so exciting. But when that happened it was never in the context of decision making. I may have thought and said you were crazy for wanting to do this or that, but I never said you *cannot* do it. I admit I was wrong as often, perhaps more often, than I was right. But the book is another cup of tea. As I said, there are no conditions that will allow me to put my name on this book unless it is in the shape I can go along with. I am sure that you know that you will have every opportunity to yell and scream as long as you want. But in the event we cannot reach agreement, I am telling you right now that I will make the final decision. If there is no unanimity on that point, let's forget the book, and each of us write what he wants to write in his own way. Give it thought."

I presented this anecdote only as a basis for making a point I consider crucial: even if I had not said what I did, the chances were near zero that I would ever have to make a "final decision," because of the degree of *trust and respect* (and affection) we had developed for each other. No one would have been in doubt that his opinion would be listened to, heard, digested, and discussed. Then why did I say it? Because if you can prevent a predictable problem from having undue, divisive effects, however small the chances, you take what you hope is an appropriate preventive stance; that is, you put the stance on the table, its letter and spirit. Articulating the letter is the easy part; the quality of relationships and outcomes depends on the spirit conveyed by the words trust and respect, and it is that spirit that is and will be absent when parent-community involvement begins to be taken seriously (there are and will be exceptions, there always are). I do not say that because I believe people are normally stubborn, perverse, and oppositional but rather because everything we know about school-community, professional-nonprofessional relationships (in the past and now) permits the prediction of problems among which the absence of trust and respect is the most troublesome. If it takes no special wisdom to make that prediction, why is it then that I have observed no instance, and I have been told of no instance, where issues of trust and respect have been stated *or even alluded to*. That is not explainable, except in rare instances, by sheer ignorance of the existence of the problem. It is explainable by the fact that the participants know the problem exists but would rather not talk about it (i.e., it is a can of worms best left unopened). Better a charade than a drama of seemingly endless conflict.

We are used to hearing that most of the problems I have been discussing are, like most other interpersonal problems, "communication" problems. I disagree. Most of the time the communication is unverbalized but crystal clear: "This is my turf, not yours," and/or "Let's agree *not* to talk about what is bothering us." You do not have to put those statements into words for their import to be "communicated." School faculty meetings are a bottomless source of examples. I cannot refrain from saying that too frequently our unverbalized messages are communicated very well, so well as to make being with each other the opposite of rewarding.

I said earlier that I do not have *an* answer to the question of how the decision making should be organized, who should have what role about what kinds of educational decisions. If I do not have an answer, I do have a starting point: a confronting and discussion of the predictable problems that can or will arise *in any group*, the members of which vary in terms of status, power, professionalism, and acquaintance with each other. To avoid that confronting and discussion at the very beginning is akin to a boxer beginning the first round by walking out and keeping his hands down and chin out. It took several months of that kind of confronting and discussion to reach agreement in 1787 about our Constitution. The founding fathers sought to build a nation, compared to which forging parents-school-community relationships is, in some ultimate sense, small potatoes. In substantive problems and principle the two are similar, if not identical.

As I pointed out at the end of the previous chapter, *the issues I have raised and discussed are as relevant to relationships between and among personnel strata in the school and school system as they are to parent-school relationships.*[2] I shall return to this again in a later chapter.

From what I have said in this chapter, it is obvious, I hope, that issues contained in the degree, scope, and the conduct-process of parental-community involvement are quite complex—unless, of course, you have that cast of mind that permits you to believe that the future will be a carbon copy of the present, and, therefore, the issues I have raised are but fads that will fade away, leaving the public schools pretty much as they are. That I consider such a head-in-the-sand belief as unrealistic goes without saying. The

---

[2] It is no different in regard to how the "constitution" governing a classroom is developed, a point I have discussed in three books (Sarason, 1982, 1990, 1993a). At its root the political principle is an educational one, a theme that runs through the writings of John Dewey, to whom what I say in this book would be old hat. A hat may be old, but that says nothing about its serviceability.

public schools will change, and the changes will be determined by two *conceptually unrelated* factors. The first is the pace, seriousness, and sincerity with which parent-community involvement occurs. The second is the public's perception and response to failure of educational outcomes to improve, a predictable failure from my perspective. Parent-community involvement, justified as it is by the political principle, does not ensure improvement in educational outcomes; it makes *accountability* for outcomes more widespread. That involvement has the potential for improvement of those outcomes but only if it comes to focus on contexts that make for productive learning, which is another way of saying that it will raise and confront this question: why are most classrooms boring and uninteresting places for students? That question does not derive from the rationale of the political principle, a fact that parent-community advocates ignore and too many educators gloss over even though in their heart of hearts they know that to be the case. So, if I cannot predict how schools will change, I can predict that how they will change will be determined by how those two factors get played out. I have been used to saying in regard to schools that the more things change the more they remain the same. I have had to change my mind. Schools will not remain the same; the changes will be for good or for bad depending on how those presently unrelated factors get interconnected.

It may be helpful to the reader if I indicate how labeling and asset-deficit issues got clarified in my mind, and by *clarified* I mean that what I had long "sensed" (i.e., vaguely) was brought into sharp focus. It was over twenty years ago when a colleague, a professional educator, said he wanted to arrange a meeting between me and a middle-aged woman who had read some of my writings and wanted to discuss them with me. She was, he said, without any professional credentials but had long been interested in and given of her time to school and other community projects. She was, he added, a person of strong convictions, especially in regard to prevailing conceptions and uses of helping services. I agreed to the meeting for two reasons:

the request was from a colleague, and I have a rule that I will see *any-one* who wants to see me. Frankly, I expected that she would have questions about which she thought I could be of help to her; I did *not* expect to be enlightened by her ideas and experience. So I met with Elizabeth Lorentz. I shall not try to describe that encounter, and it was an encounter because she challenged some of my ideas; she did not come hat-in-hand, so to speak, to be enlightened by a Yale professor. She liked my writings, she said, but I was fuzzy on two crucial points. The first was that despite the fact that I was trying to direct attention to the prevention of problems, to the futility of depending exclusively on a clinical-repair approach to the problems of people, I tended to see the problems of individuals too much in terms of what they did not know or could not do. I was, she said most politely, not predisposed to look beyond their deficits to their assets. And it was only by building on assets that you could be help-ful. The second point was in the form of example after example from schools and other agencies illustrating how the assets of individuals, despite their deficits, could be used to increase and bolster the assets of others (i.e., resource exchange). She liked my emphasis on the fact that resources are always limited, but I did not, she said, see as clearly as I should that the deficit orientation exacerbated the prob-lem of limited resources. She was not, I should hasten to say, "attack-ing" me; she felt a kinship with me and that I would take her remarks seriously, that I would feel a kinship with her. What was dispiriting to her was that she concluded from her "volunteer" expe-riences, which were the opposite of minuscule, that the helping pro-fessions (including education) were so "deficit oriented" in their conceptions and practices that she saw no light at the end of the tunnel. She felt intellectually alone. (She was the mentor of Dr. Richard Sussman whom I discussed earlier in this chapter in the use of high school seniors, and that was only one of many similar exam-ples I could have drawn from his and her experience.)

That meeting with Elizabeth Lorentz was of the "aha" genre: she had posed and I saw the deficit-asset issues more clearly than before. It also mightily reinforced my rule that I will see anyone who wants to see me!

There is a postscript to that meeting. Elizabeth had learned that two people in the medical school were planning a large community project from a preventive orientation, and from a preliminary paper they had written it seemed as if they were guided by ideas similar to hers. Did I know them and could I arrange for her to meet with them? I knew them and I arranged the meeting. It was an interpersonal disaster. They were patronizing and smug and made it quickly apparent that they did not feel they had anything to learn from *her*. They listened but heard nothing. They were the experts; she was a layperson. Elizabeth was one of the four people who most influenced my intellectual development. None was a psychologist, which is not to say that I have not been influenced by other psychologists.[3]

Let me conclude with an experience concomitant with the writing of this chapter. I was consulting to a project in Tucson that seeks to bring about change in a school where almost all the children are of Mexican origin, a fair number who speak only Spanish or are not at home with English; their families are poor (many very poor) and educational outcomes what you would expect. The project was conceived and initiated four years ago by Dr. Paul Heckman of the University of Arizona in Tucson. This project, one of the two I have found fascinating, instructive, and encouraging, is in the process of being written up for publication. I shall briefly discuss two of its aspects. The first is that from its inception it was made explicit that the university personnel would *not* assume the responsibility for telling anyone how and in what ways the school should change. That responsibility would be assumed and dis-

---

[3] For the reader who may be interested in these four people, I describe them and their influence in greater detail in *The Making of an American Psychologist* (1988). Whatever the virtues of professional education, and they are not to be derogated, they are inevitably parochial in their effects, making it very difficult for those within the profession to become aware that his or her way of looking at things may have some shaky underpinnings.

charged by teachers, parents, and relevant social agencies; they would, in Dr. Heckman's words, "reinvent" the school. What I found refreshing and fascinating about that concept and approach was an undergirding assumption: those groups had the assets to change the school in ways they thought necessary and desirable. As I observed and was predictable (both to Dr. Heckman and me) was that these groups were so accustomed to believing that the school's salvation would come from "outsiders" other than themselves that they had inordinate difficulty seeing themselves as possessing assets. They wanted direction, to be told what the school should be and how to bring that about. But Dr. Heckman and his colleagues did not fall into the trap of agreeing with their self-perceptions; it was not easy. I observed transformations in parents that are difficult to put into words, but, fortunately, some of these transformations are on video- and audiotapes, and that is also the case for the teachers. The school has been reinvented, which is not to say that an educational paradise exists in the Ochoa elementary school. If I needed any confirmation (I always need it!) of the productiveness of the asset orientation, that project has provided it.

That brings me to the bilingual problem in that school. Before my last visit there in February 1994, I learned that the teachers and parents had decided to put into the same classroom students who spoke only Spanish, those who spoke Spanish but had some proficiency in English, and some who knew no Spanish and spoke English only. Gaining commitment (from parents and others) was not easy but it was gained, and with the result that students, in the countless ways they interact with each other, began informally to "teach" each other so that English-speaking students were "picking up" Spanish and vice versa. I know little about bilingual education except that it is an arena in which opposing conceptions arouse controversy and passion. In the course of the visit I interviewed two of the project staff who can be validly described as very knowledgeable in this particular field. One was Anna Loebe, a graduate student, a former teacher, and of Mexican origin. The other was

Howard Smith, an advanced graduate student, African American, and completely fluent in Spanish. My interaction with each of these unusual individuals was not for the purpose of obtaining their observations of the school's bilingual classes but rather to have them inform me about what was going on in the field generally. In his or her own way each said, "If a child cannot speak English, that child is labeled as having a deficit. It is impossible for most people, including teachers, to see that child as having an asset useful to others." It was as if each of them had somehow heard my first encounter with Elizabeth Lorentz and they had drawn the appropriate conclusion.

I said that the problems are complex, a term that suggests that we know there are a lot of variables in the picture, and we are not sure we know how they are interconnected. I prefer the term *messy* as recognition of the fact that there are variables relevant to educational process and purpose that are missing from the picture, but few seem willing or able to put them into the picture. If those variables are not in the picture but continue to brew and reinforce the problems for which the picture is intended to serve as a guide for action, we are truly in a mess, a complex mess. In the next chapter the messiness will increase as we turn to questions that this and the previous chapters have begged: what limits, if any, should constrain the scope of parent-community involvement? And if the reader has any doubt that the fan can blow more than air, the next chapter will erase that doubt.

Chapter Six

Beyond the Political Principle

Like the process of parent-community involvement, that of writing is unpredictable. For example, you know how you are going to start a chapter, and then "something happens" that tells you "start here, not there." The night before the morning I started this chapter, relieved that I knew how this chapter would open, I was in the company of five friends and a nine-year-old girl who, with her mother, had arrived that afternoon in Sedona, Arizona, for the first time. After some chit-chat we began, humorously, we thought, to query the mother about when she and her daughter would move to Sedona, one of the two most beautiful spots on earth (Bryce Canyon is the other—see your travel agent). After several minutes of this banter the girl (Rosa Cushman), who was sitting close to her mother and had not said a word, looked at her mother and said, "You won't move here without talking to me, would you?" To which the mother laughingly replied, "Of course not. We would not move until your brother and sister finished college and you would be ready for high school. Besides, you have to visit your father every Wednesday and Saturday and you could not do that here in Sedona." Rosa was not satisfied and said (not asked) insistingly but not anxiously, "Even then, you would not make a decision without first asking me." To the five of us (Sherry and Martin King, Pat Wasely, Rick Lear, and me) the interchange was surprising on two counts: the mother took the girl's questions seriously, as a matter of course; Rosa's questions were asked as a matter of principle (i.e., she had *rights* she expected her mother to honor). Her mother saw our surprise at the interchange and told us that Rosa was doing a year-long project on the rights of children, a project the mother had conceived and was supervising.

The conversation among all of us was longer and more substantive than I have indicated. Afterward, I took Rosa aside and said, "Rosa, you were asking the right questions for the right reasons. You expect that if a decision were to be made that would affect you—moving to a strange place far away from Massachusetts, not being able to see your father two days a week, leaving your friends and more—your feelings should in some ways, important ways, be recognized and taken into account. But let's say that they are recognized and discussed, but you can't come to an agreement. What do you do then? Who makes the decision?" Almost with no reaction time Rosa indicated *that* was a doozy of a question and she did not have an answer, but if her mother made the decision to move, it would be because she *had* to, just as the divorce between her parents *had* to take place. She assumed her mother would never make a decision that ignored Rosa's ideas, needs, feelings.

So why begin this chapter with an incident that kept me from falling asleep, as I am accustomed to, quickly? For one thing, it reminded me again how mischievous labels can be; that is, more than ever, I now regard "nine-year-olds" as possessed of assets, actual or potential, relevant to the intricacies and dilemmas of decision making. If you think of nine-year-olds as *just* nine-year-olds and react to them accordingly, you end up with "evidence" that proves your self-fulfilling prophecy, which is in principle what educators do in regard to parent-community involvement in educational decision making. For another thing, it reminded me that the issue of the rights of parents in regard to that decision making, an issue gaining force, is but one instance of rights coming to the fore in other arenas of human relationships. Within the past two years (at least) the mass media have given play to cases challenging traditional views of the rights of children vis-à-vis parents, challenges that have been and will continue to be in the courts. Just as there was a time when wives, by virtue of law and custom, had few rights compared to husbands, that was and still largely is the case between child and parents. But that too is changing, however much that may be viewed by some people as ridiculous and socially destructive. Laws, legal or judicial, are reflections of social attitudes and change; they do not have virginal births, they are outcroppings of social change the pace and consequences of which are far from predictable. One thing is clear: when a change in principle has received judicial sanction (e.g., desegregation, women's rights, etc.), its percolating effects become stronger and more widespread.

Finally, the Rosa anecdote confirms, to me at least, the conclusion that forms of involvement in decision making are in some ultimate, practical sense less important for realization of the spirit of involvement than degree and quality of the mutual trust and respect characterizing that involvement. When that involvement has all of the characteristics of a charade, of an unarticulated but experienced gulf between what is thought and what is said, of a power game the goal of which is to maintain the *status quo*, of a process geared to avoid conflict and threatening ideas—given these characteristics the failure of that involvement is something you can bet on and give odds. I have seen too many instances of mandated involvement where one or all of those characteristics were present, with results ranging from increased apathy and disinterest to open warfare. I have seen involvement I consider exemplary that arose by virtue of perceived principle and not external mandates. I am, I think, realistic enough to expect that in the vast majority of our schools meaningful involvement will not be initiated except by differing degrees of "mandates" from outside the schools or from on high within school systems. That source of initiation is both an opportunity and a trap. I will elaborate on that in later pages. These are messy problems, but, let us remind ourselves, nobody ever promised us a rose garden. We promised ourselves a rose garden, a promise that was a fateful step down the stairs of public grace.

Now to some concrete problems. A school has a curriculum. A group of parents object to the biology segment of the curriculum because it contains nothing about creationism and a good deal about Darwinian evolution, or, worse yet to them, the "scientific" view disparages the biblical explanation of how the world was created. The parents, and not infrequently there are more than parents, demand that the creationism they espouse be included in the curriculum. A familiar situation, one that almost always engenders conflict that often spills over to election of members of the board of education, hiring of school personnel, and firing some existing administrators and teachers.

I shall assume that no reader will deny that these parents have a right to believe in creationism as an explanation of how the world began. But do they have a right to request or demand (1) that the curriculum contain no disparagement of their belief and/or (2) that their belief should be part of the curriculum? In my opinion, on the basis of the political principle they have such rights. If a group of parents (or even one parent) concludes that a decision has been or will be made that in their view adversely affects their interests and beliefs, that view should in some way at some time be represented in the decision-making process. That such representation-participation may be viewed by you as silly, costly in time, potentially divisive in consequences, by your lights antieducational and antiscientific, and a blurring of the lines between church and state is irrelevant to the question of the right to be heard. I would go so far as to say that to deny them that right is an instance of intolerance.

If I justify such representation-participation, on what conceptions of learning and education can I respond respectfully and seriously to what they ask? The political principle speaks to participation-representation, *not* to the pros and cons of substantive issues, and in regard to those issues the principle is no guide. So, from this point on (in this instance) we are not concerned with that principle. What I (we) must be concerned with is how, if at all, we can justify creationism in the curriculum and reexamining whether that curriculum does indeed disparage alternative views. Put in another way, believing as I personally do that creationism is an inadequate way of explaining the origins of the world, far less explanatory than the Darwinian one, can I nevertheless justify exposing students to creationism on educational grounds? My answer is yes and for several reasons.

If an aim of education is to broaden and deepen a student's knowledge and grasp of human behavior and history in general and our society in particular, it is impossible to do so without understanding the role of religions (plural, not singular). It is possible, of course, but only at the expense of facts and truths, and how more antieducational can you get? We are a society of many religions, some of which (Christian, Judaic, Moslem, Mormon) have identical views of creationism but many others that do not, particularly those that developed in Africa and the Far East, and let us not forget Native Americans (which we have managed to do rather well). This diversity of views is a fact, in our present and past, and for those holding any of these views it is also a guide for living, a kind of moral compass for making sense of the world. If that is an indisputable fact, it is a fact that becomes a problem *only* when one group seeks to foist their view on others or disparage or punish those with a different view, which is why our founding fathers guaranteed the separation of church and state, and it is why teaching creationism in the public schools should not be presented in a disparaging way but literally as a fact. That is, creationism is not of a piece; it is differently viewed by the different religions. If a child goes to a Christian, Jewish, Mormon, or Moslem school in our country, it should not surprise us if that child is indoctrinated in *a* point of view. If I understand the purpose of that indoctrination, it in no way means that that indoctrination meets my criteria of the purposes of education, among the most important of which is broadening understanding of the world we live in *together*. That is the purpose of the public school, a purpose easy to state, easy to accept, but extraordinarily difficult to achieve in ways consistent with that purpose.

Darwin's work, theory, and writings did not deal with how the world was created and by whom but with the origins of species.

Nevertheless, his work and that of his scientific descendants present a view of evolution clearly different from that of *any* religious view of the origins of the world. *There is as much difference between and among some religious conceptions of creation as there is between Darwinian evolution and any one religious view.* What distinguishes Darwinian theory from religious conceptions has been the range of phenomena it explains, the predictions it generated and proved, the puzzles it has unraveled, and the questions it has raised about diversity masking a unity. Darwin's theory is and remains a theory but one for which validating data are abundant. For a public school student to be ignorant of evolutionary theory is as inexcusable as being ignorant of the circulation of the blood.

When parents request or demand the teaching of creationism it raises (for me) educational issues, not religious ones, requiring (of me) a kind of soul searching about what I want students to know about themselves, others, and our wondrous, frustrating world, ruled as it should be by the maxim that the more you know the more you need to know. So, it would be hypocritical of me summarily to reject parental requests for the teaching of creationism because in my opinion Darwinian theory is an infinitely more valid explanation of phenomena than are competing theories. It would be no less hypocritical if in justifying teaching of creationism I was agreeing to "equal time," to a watering down of the exposure to Darwinian theory. There is a difference between accommodating to a point of view and mindlessly succumbing to it. Assuming that you take the political principle seriously, and assuming that you are aware that truth is a many-splendored thing, and further assuming that you are able (as an educator you should be) to think of issues in terms of educational purposes, you are still left with the question, How do I (we) decide the issue? In the "real world" you will decide it on the basis of the size and strength of a supportive constituency you are obliged to make knowledgeable about the educational issues involved, a constituency you (should) have reason to believe is a representative sample of the community. Constituency building (and maintenance) is the name of the game, and by that I do not mean that constituencies are developed to insure that your stance, and only your stance, "wins" out. Anyone who does not know that schools are in, part of, impacted on by the political system also believes in the tooth fairy.

But there is another factor that complicates matters. If the decision is to include creationism, you have the obligation to put on the table the realities of children, teachers, and classroom, realities that are predictable. Let us assume that the teacher makes every effort to present creationism and Darwinism as dispassionately as possible, regardless of his or her views on these matters. Children are children, which means they are question-asking organisms. What if, by virtue of differences in family background and religious affiliation, children begin debating with and criticizing each others' view or, as likely, pressing the teacher to state his or her views? Unlike the substance of math or chemistry, children from a very early age wrestle with questions about how the world came about, who or what was the primal force, just as they ask questions (if only to themselves) about conception, birth, and sex differences. In a classroom in which question asking as a way of seeking and digesting knowledge has been encouraged, the issues we have been discussing will engender lively give and take, as indeed it should. That is putting the teacher in a difficult (very difficult) position. Should the teacher, when pressed, say he or she has no position, which, of course, no child in the classroom would believe? Should he or she say she has a position but does not want to influence others, to which some students will wonder why the teacher does not trust them to make up their own minds? If a student intolerantly puts down another student for having a different view, will the parents of that intolerant child understand when their child tells them at dinner that his views were criticized, not his intolerance? The possibilities are many, as are the sources of misunderstanding. Unless parents are made more knowledgeable about classroom dynamics, and alerted to the predictability and complexity of those dynamics, and the moral-educational tight rope on which the teacher is walking, you are asking for trouble. Committing those errors of omission is to overlook a process in which mutual trust and respect stands a chance of being achieved.

The point of what I have been saying is severalfold. First, there is no justification for not giving a respectful and serious hearing to parents. Second, if the parental request or demand comes as a surprise, it means you did not know the community, you did not act preventively, and you put yourself in the repair mode. Third, your response has to be in terms of educational process and goals that are clear, defensible, and nonpersonal. Fourth, you must never expect that a process derived from the political principle will be other than time-consuming, on the surface inefficient, its outcomes often unpredictable, and the timing and art of compromise should always be in the wings, clearly distinguishable from unprincipled caving in. Fifth, it is a process for which you, whatever your assets of knowledge and experience, may be temperamentally unsuited.

I am, I think, sufficiently in touch with events to expect that some readers will say that what I have left out in this story about creationism is that its proponents often have an agenda and possess attitudes they do not put on the table. That is to say, creationism is but an outcropping of a congeries of attitudes and feelings toward schools as places where educators conspire to indoctrinate students with values antithetical to those of family, true patriotism, and the spiritual life. They thoroughly distrust the motives of educators whom they see as rank materialists, devotees of any new fad or fashion that undervalues (if not subverts) the acquirement of facts, skills, and knowledge (the "basics")—that is, the polar opposite of what these parents say they experienced when they were students. For them the classroom is a place where students are expected to do and learn what they are told, no ifs, ands, or buts; it is a place in which continuity in unquestioned tradition is instilled and reinforced. They recognize that the world has changed in ways they oppose, but that is all the more reason that schools should be places where students are inoculated to those changes. Escalating rates of

crime, drugs, untraditional lifestyles, "sexual freedom," teenage pregnancy, zooming rates of divorce—all of these and more are viewed
by them as symptoms of a national, Babylonian decline to which
schools are contributing.

I have talked to enough of those who hold these views, and I
have read a good deal of the literature they circulate, to feel secure
in my description of their feelings, attitudes, conclusions, and proposals. Indeed, on a couple of occasions, I have articulated their position to them in order to determine whether I was distorting their
views; they said I was surprisingly on target. That was no surprise to
me because I was merely repeating what they had said and written.

There are two questions here. (There are more than two, but
the two are more central to this book.) How should we think about
these views? How do we respond to them? Let us start with the first
question.

Granted that the views I described above are extreme, it
would be a mistake to regard their proponents as atypically dissatisfied with our schools. Put in another way, many people and
for different reasons are dissatisfied with our schools. We hear, of
course, from *organized* groups of dissatisfied parents but, as school
personnel know well, there are many parents who, again for one
or another reason, are critical of schools.[1] To deny that this is the

---

[1] On the front page of the *Arizona Republic* was the headline "House Bows on Home
Schooling." The article begins as follows:

Washington—The House of Representatives, besieged by thousands of telephone calls and faxes, retreated Thursday from a measure that home-school
advocates had feared would threaten parents' right to teach their children at
home.

The house overwhelmingly approved two amendments designed to reas-
sure home schoolers that an education-aid bill would not undermine their
independence.

"We've shown we will fight for our freedoms," said a relieved Mike Farris, president of the Virginia-based Home School Legal Defense Association.
"Congress wrote something that was clearly dangerous."

Farris estimated that between 600,000 and 1 million children—including 10,000 to 15,000 in Arizona—are educated at home.

case is inexcusable. Nor is it excusable to say that there always have been and will always be dissatisfied parents. The question we cannot avoid is why their numbers are not small. Just as it is flagrantly unjust and an indulgence of ignorance to blame schools for everything amiss in our society, it is similarly so to blame parents for the problems school personnel encounter in teaching uninterested, unmotivated, behaviorally difficult children, varying widely in ability and/or performance, all in the same classroom with "good" students. That kind of blame assignment virtually guarantees that the dissatisfaction on both sides will continue and fester. The most frequent (I would say universal) explanation offered by educators is that parents simply do not understand the complexity of the teacher's role, the consequences of wide diversity among students, finishing a curriculum by a certain date, why the class day is divided up the way it is, what principals do, why they so frequently feel between a rock and a hard place, how teachers are evaluated and by whom, and more. Yes, if parents are ignorant of these matters it is very likely that their dissatisfactions—be they about their child, the curriculum, the teacher, homework (too much or too little), grading, report cards, standards—may strike you as unwarranted, at best, and sheer ignorance, at worst, or somewhere in between. *But if parents "do not understand," is it not, in part at least, because educators have been woefully negligent about seriously "educating" parents about classrooms, schools, roles, pressures, constraints?* This is in no way to suggest that the goal is to transform parents into sophisticated educators. But it is to suggest that, generally speaking, parents are perfectly capable of absorbing explanations if, as one parent put it, "I'm not being given the party line; I am not seen as a child entitled to no opinions, as if my asking questions is irritatingly intrusive, as if the way things are is the best of all possible ways, as if there really is nothing to discuss, as if I should only focus on my child and anything else about the school is none of my business." That was said by one of my physicians, a young woman quite atypical in her opinions about the too-frequent tendency of physicians to talk to patients as if they had empty heads, or if there was something in their heads, it should not be cluttered with information they could not understand or would inevitably distort. The self-fulfilling prophecy is alive and well in and beyond the educational arena!

Over the decades I have learned a lot from teachers who were parents. Here, briefly, is how a fair number described how they felt after meeting with their child's teacher, or principal, or the school psychologist. Unlike ordinary parents, of course, they did not regard themselves as amateurs; they were peers. In all instances (if memory serves me right) it was the parent who initiated the meeting.

1. The parent approached the meeting with unease and dysphoric anticipation, as if she (all shes) knew the teacher would "feel on the spot."

2. The parent felt she was regarded as a "know-it-all."

3. Without saying it in so many words, the teacher implied that the parent's view of the particular issue was a prejudiced one (i.e., the parent had a one-sided view, while the teacher saw things whole).

4. The suggestions of the parent were reacted to by what may be termed a "you stay on your turf and I'll stay on mine" stance. The parent was made to feel she was being intrusive, directive.

5. In instances where there was no meeting of minds, the teacher's facial and body language seemed to say, "You are being contentious."

6. Throughout the meeting the parent was poignantly aware of the danger of putting her child in between two warring camps (i.e., if the parent said what she really thought, her child might be adversely affected).

It should be said that none of the parents generalized their reactions to all teachers or other personnel. But it also has to be said that these parents were in no doubt that many personnel were not at ease with parents, did not trust them to the point where they could be spontaneous, revealing, and admit error or imperfection.

It is not an unjust extrapolation to say that these instances tell us a good deal about why parent-school relationships are as unproductive as they frequently are; why parents approach school personnel with a mixture of respect, deference, fear, and anger; why trust is such a rare commodity in these relationships; why school personnel believe that keeping parents at a distance is less troublesome than sincerely involving them. On this last point educators could not be more realistic in the sense that once you take parent-community involvement seriously life becomes more complicated, messy, and even more unpredictable than it was before. That life can *become* more interesting, exciting, less isolating, protective of the existence of the public schools, and potentially an aid to their improvement is a goal and possibility educators have difficulty envisioning. And that is what is called for: a vision that pulls us to a future, not one riveted on a present satisfactory to few.

Several criticisms will be directed to what I have said in this chapter. The first is that I began the chapter describing groups who in their heart of hearts would love to dismantle the public schools, and then I seemed to change course and assign blame to educators for the gulf between them and parent-community groups. The criticism is both right and wrong. It is wrong in the sense that in no way did I imply that the gulf was willed, as if educators conspired to bring the situation about, as if they revel in the way things are, as if they are more mired in their parochial outlook than any other professional group. The present situation has a long history in American society and culture, waves of immigrations, the emergence of public schools, compulsory education, and what has been termed (not only in regard to education) the cult of professionalism. In brief, a tradition developed in which successive generations of educators were socialized and that seemed to "work" until World War II set the stage for the era of *rights*.

The criticism is right in that the profession of education, no less and no more than any other profession, has been awfully slow to become sensitive to the issues of rights, in particular the political principle, and even slower to begin sincerely, courageously, and seriously to alter its professional traditions. It is the lack of meaningful response, the lack of articulate leadership that are my basis for assigning blame. To understand all is not to forgive all.

The second criticism is that I have fallen into the trap of placing still another obligation-burden on school personnel, one that will be costly in time and effort. It is a familiar story that schools have been required to do *something* about *almost all* important social problems (e.g., drugs, smoking, sex, teenage pregnancy, driver education, juvenile crime, AIDS, and a lot more). Clearly, if educators take the political principle (and its derivative issues) seriously, time, the most precious of commodities, will become far more of a problem than it is. My answer is that schools can be justly criticized for lack of clarity about priorities and the lack of courage to resist taking on programs that further obscure the issue of priorities. Communities have required schools to initiate programs, to help "solve" racial problems, *at the same time they are dissatisfied with what schools accomplish in other matters educational.* You could argue that to be consistent with the political principle and parent-community involvement, I am not entitled to criticize schools when they initiate programs parents and others want and educators may or may not want. I agree. But my criticism is not that schools took on these programs but that they did so without an effort to engage the community in the issues of priorities *and* existing educational inadequacies; that is, the community was provided no basis for judging between and among educational priorities and problems. It was too often the case of knowing the price of everything and the value of nothing. It was hard to figure out what educators stood for. And, I must remind the reader of what I have said earlier about the political principle: taking it seriously in no way means that the outcomes of the process will always be salutary. But it does mean that the important issues stand a chance of getting on the table. Concretely, and from my standpoint, the most important issue is in the form of this question: when a child is graduated from high school, what are the one or two characteristics you want that child to possess, characteristics previous schooling has reinforced? All else is commentary. This will become more clear in the penultimate chapter where it will become apparent that however sincerely I advocate for parent-community involvement, it will ultimately have to be judged by how educators and parents respond to the question I have just asked. You cannot answer a question you have not raised. But the question has been raised many times before. Neither educators nor the public have taken it seriously. And, here again, I place major responsibility on the education profession because they know that the question is the central one that practice has to reflect. Ironically, in the many times I have raised the question with parent groups, I have gotten two reactions, without exception: the first is puzzled (and long) silence about how to answer the question, and second, after I have broken the silence with *my* answer, they wholeheartedly agreed with me. That may come as a surprise to many educators; they have far more kinship to parental goals than the gulf between them indicates.

The third criticism is that I obviously never have had to confront parent groups so prejudiced, so narrow, so critical as to make discussion an exercise in futility; they are literally intolerant, incapable of entertaining the possibility they are wholly or in large measure wrong, unable to respect your right to your position, which they interpret as a reflection of a personal-moral deficit on your part, or a "radical" intent on changing the world in subversive ways. Why is *Catcher in the Rye* in the school library? Why are you supporting (or not supporting) giving condoms to students? Why are you advocating a curriculum that approves (or seems to approve) wildly different life, family, sexual styles? Why do history and social studies texts criticize the United States? Why are you trying to get African American students to talk English English, disparaging and punishing their use of accustomed black dialect? Why is the history of my ethnic group, its history of sordid experience of discrimination, not in the curriculum? Each of these is a legitimate question but not when it is asked on a "take it and *you* leave" basis, "there is nothing to discuss," and the unverbalized conclusion "you ain't seen nothing yet!" There are times when discussion is fruitless, an exercise in masochism, and where the outcome will be decided on the size and strength of the informed constituency you have built up over the years, a constituency you developed not to have their votes in your pocket but because you and they forged a tradition of mutual trust and respect through no-holds-barred discussion in which substantive issues, not power ones, were the focus, where you learned from them and they learned from you. If you get into constituency development after the bomb has been put in place and a match to set it off has been lit, the outcome may have already been decided. Let me elaborate on the basis of recent events in Connecticut.[2]

In 1992, on the basis of legislative action, the governor appointed a Commission on Educational Excellence for Connecticut. It issued its report January 31, 1994. Here is a letter published in a local newspaper, written by Edward Meyer who was a high school teacher for eighteen years, a college teacher for eight years, with ten years' experience in chemical and allied industries. He dubs himself (correctly) Minister of Responsible Disturbance. Here is his letter in its entirety (Meyer, 1994):

> To the Editor:
>
> This letter is a recommendation to voters that we collectively oppose adoption of the recommendations in *The Report of the Commission on Educational Excellence for Connecticut* (Jan. 31, 1994), at least temporarily, for these reasons.

---

[2] I urge the reader to read what I consider a great American novel, *The Last Hurrah* by Edwin O'Connor. The movie based on the novel was terrible (that may be a slight exaggeration, so let us say it deserved one star on a five-star scale). No one I know who read the book was prepared for the last ten to twenty pages because only there, after supersophisticated Skeffington has lost the election, does it become apparent why he lost: he had lost touch with the fact that new constituencies had come on the scene, constituencies that potentially could have been supportive but to whom he paid no attention.

(1) During the 18 months the Commission functioned, we the public were invited only once—one night, in a few towns during the January freeze, from 7 PM, to comment on the results. Members of the public were given a few crumbs of remaining time after organization representatives presented their view. This did not allow enough time for the Commission to successfully explain its proposals to the public; nor did it allow adequate time, either for the public to make its voice heard, or for the Commission to reflect upon the public commentary that was received.

(2) These sentiments (published in the Commission-Report) from State Senator James Maloney, (assistant majority leader and Senate Chair of the Finance, Revenue and Bonding Committee), who also noted: (pp. 52–53) "The Commission's rush at the end distorted its own internal process. During the first 15 months of work, the Commission deliberated with great care and with complete respect for the opinions of every member. In the final three months, there was very regrettable over-reliance on parliamentary procedure and divisive vote-taking. During the full Commission discussion of the key features of the school funding formula . . . the debate was prematurely cut short by a motion to call the question. The full Commission debated the entire formula issue for less than six hours in the full eighteen months and then found it necessary to end the debate precipitously."

Is it reasonable for voters to support recommendations based on necessary expenditures for programs about which the revenue uncertainties are matched by lack of knowledge and understanding of what the revenues will pay for?

(3) The Weicker-appointed 43-member Commission was asked to study current policies and practices in the state's education system and recommend changes required to establish and maintain a truly world-class education system with opportunity available to all students. In their letter accompanying the Report, Co-chairmen William Connolly and Education Commissioner Vincent Far-

randino wrote, ". . . Most importantly, the public at large must be brought into any successful process of education reform."

(4) In Governor Weicker's "State of the State" address (Feb. 9) he correctly forewarned, "   You will hear much venom and falsehood. You will hear attacks on the Commission's work, claiming it supports 'outcome-based education,' a phrase detractors have seized on to describe everything that is wrong with America today. You will hear regional planning described as 'forced busing' and 'end of local control.' You will hear these and other lies, but I ask you this: Do not give the fearmongers the gift of your attention. There is too much at stake."

The voices described by the Governor are the modern version of Luddites, people who rebelled destructively when they were threatened by the Industrial Revolution in the 19th Century. Their voices have a right to be heard in open public discussion, debate, questions, suggestions, anger, approval, criticism to help clarify the issues. The Commission has ignored these needs, thus far.

There is no doubt—Connecticut public schools must do much better. We need well-educated citizens capable of more than merely beating the kids of other nations in the competitive market place during their adult years. Public participation is vital, lest we, by default, become victims.

Carol Rocque, head of the Excellence Commission, PO Box 2219, Hartford CT 96145 can supply a copy of the very readable Report. Or call 566–8889 (FAX 566–8890) your request. Before we approve legislative consideration of these recommendations, let us first be heard all over Connecticut.

Sincerely,

Edward Meyer

When his letter was published in a local newspaper, Mr. Meyer—a dear friend who is part of my counterintelligence network— received calls from several newspapers around the state. Why?

Because at the few public hearings the commission held, its report was scathingly criticized by many people, including one by a group I will discuss shortly. It would be an exaggeration to say all hell had broken loose at the several public hearings, so let us just say they were stormy, replete with criticism ranging from lack of time for discussion to accusing the commission of foisting on the public an "Outcomes Based" ideology that would subvert American ideals, values, and schools (as Governor Weicker had said in the excerpt Mr. Meyer quoted).

The point of the story is an ironic one. One of the Commission's recommendations is as follows (*The Report of the Commission on Educational Excellence for Connecticut*, 1994):

> Districts should establish formal, written school policies to: keep parents informed of and involved in the educational progress of their children; help parents support and sustain the values of education and the expectation that learning is the primary responsibility of every student; and support organized and meaningful parent involvement in every school—including parent participation in school decision-making and efforts to assure that schools and classrooms are open and welcoming to parents.

Another recommendation:

> Actions should be taken to implement the provisions of an existing statute that calls for the creation of model programs to encourage parent support, participation, and responsibility as partners in the education of their children.

Two more recommendations:

> Parents should be assured of reasonable time off from work to attend school conferences and activities; school personnel should make concerted efforts to be accessible beyond their regular workdays to the families of the children they serve.
>
> Skills for creating successful parent involvement should be

incorporated into teacher and administrator preparation programs, certification, and continuing education opportunities.

The irony inheres in the fact that although the commission clearly accepts the political principle, its own way of involving parents and others in discussing its report was a blatant violation of the spirit of the principle. "Do not give the fearmongers the gift of your attention"—those words by Governor Weicker seemed to have been taken seriously by the commission. To give your attention is no gift, it is a responsibility, however much you regard criticisms as uninformed, misleading, unwarranted, and symptomatic of a "Luddite" posture. Since I accept the maxim that it is hard to be completely wrong, a maxim the governor obviously rejects, I assume that the "fearmongers" may be raising one or two legitimate points. And that brings me to the Concerned Women of America (CWOA), a militant, highly organized, politically conservative, superpatriotic group that was represented very articulately at some, if not at all, of the commission's meetings (as were La Rouche supporters).

One of the publications of CWOA is titled *Outcome Based Education: Remaking Your Children Through Radical Reform*.[3] I hold no brief for outcome based education (OBE) for several reasons. I recoil at any *seemingly* new approach that promises the world. Second, in the different versions I have read they have one thing in common: they are written on a level of generality that serves as no guide for action-implementation, guaranteeing a degree of diversity that may or may not be appropriate, productive, or permit judgments (let alone studies) of comparability. Diversity is not inherently a virtue. Third, there is no recognition whatsoever about the *predictable* problems OBE will encounter and has encountered. Fourth, there is no recognition that OBE contains nothing new in terms of ideas, values, goals, a lack that is not lethal but makes me wonder why its proponents think its time has come—that is, why the ideas it espouses did not "take" in the past,

---

[3]This publication can be obtained from Concerned Women of America, 370 L'Enfant Promenade, N.W., Suite 800, Washington, D.C. 20024.

what obstacles they encountered, and why they are any less thorny now. For example, OBE is critical, and rightly so, of the use of traditional standardized tests as the primary decision-making basis for determining a student's educational-intellectual progress and instead advocates means for determining not only what a student knows or has learned but whether that student can *apply*—by individually tailored projects, exhibits, or portfolios—what he or she has learned. Acquired knowledge that is inapplicable to the life and realities of students is not only arid knowledge but eminently and quickly forgotten, as all readers of this book know. John Dewey wrote about this a hundred years ago.

When you read and hear the attacks of CWOA on OBE, it is hard—for me it is impossible—to avoid the conclusion that OBE is seen as the educational equivalent of Russia's "Evil Empire" in the days of the cold war; that is, the enemy is at our schools' doors, the nation is asleep, and CWOA in the tradition of Paul Revere is waking us up. Never has so much been attributed to so little. But in one respect CWOA explicitly raises a very important point: what evidence is there that deemphasizing standardized tests and instead using "performance-based" data (e.g., portfolios, exhibits) will be more productive or valid or control for the subjectivity of judgment? That is a legitimate question. It is an act of faith on my part to believe that what OBE is advocating *potentially* can be a far better means for judging what a student has learned and can apply than relying on achievement test scores. But I also know two things: there is no evidence at present that it is a better means, and the research to demonstrate its superiority will be difficult and long.[4] If at the point of a gun I *had* to choose between standardized tests and

---

[4] I have had the opportunity to visit three high schools, each over two days, in different parts of the country. In each school there was a serious effort to use exhibits and portfolios by students to stimulate and capitalize on his or her interests as a way of acquiring knowledge, skills, and a sense of personal-intellectual competence and independence. As one would expect, a small minority of students achieved these goals; the

alternative means, I would choose the latter, but only at the point of a gun. I resent the "hard sell" that confuses hope with accomplishment. I am not advocating waiting until the research evidence is compelling, if only because the standardized tests are, more often than not, misused, or misinterpreted, or mindlessly given significance for policy and action that, at best, are unjustified and, at worst, a complete waste of time, and usually it is both. So, CWOA is not completely wrong, although they come very close as I shall now indicate. The CWOA is a clear example of what educators can be up against when they take the political principle seriously. How do you deal with individuals and groups who view educators as subversive of all that this country stands for, as solely responsible for every social ill in our society?

In their publication on OBE the CWOA says the following:

> Reinforcing the call for social upheaval, Education Week's editors note Dr. Sarason [of Yale University] likens the changes that are needed to the founding of the U.S. government. "Education Week's editors have sought to demonstrate that there is a consensus among education experts—whether from state or Ivy League universities—that the United States must pave the way for the 'new era' by ushering in a radical social transformation. Advocating wide scale reform—cultural, social, and political, as well as educational—Education Week's editors, serving as mouthpieces for OBE proponents, attempt to lead the reader to conclude that there is no viable alternative."

---

large majority did not. To achieve these goals requires a degree of quality of supervision, and time of teachers, which were in short supply. That should not be interpreted as an argument to continue to use standardized tests.

It is an argument for understanding far better than we now do how to answer the question: what are the *minimal* conditions that would permit more students to obtain the benefits of these kinds of individual projects? That is a question the advocates of OBE have not asked, just as proponents of standardized tests do not ask: what are these tests *not* telling us?

Note that the writer does not quote me but rather one sentence from a few contained in an article. Note also that the one sentence has a kernel of truth in that in several of my books (including this one) I use the constitutional convention of 1787 as an instructive instance of a *process* for coming to grips with basic issues and problems. Apparently, the writer for CWOA concluded that since I regarded the 1787 convention with awe and respect, I am in favor of another convention, the purpose of which is to undo the first revolution and to start the second one. And, since I was being quoted in *Education Week*, and that publication seemed to endorse OBE, they concluded that I was in favor of social upheaval for which OBE was but one line of revolutionary attack. (I have never written a single word about OBE until this chapter.) I was guilty by association, for being an Ivy League professor; for regarding the 1787 convention as one of the momentous events in human history; for being an "education expert"; and for being deceitful, subversive, and, I suppose, just plain stupid. For the CWOA there is truth and untruth, and guess who has the monopoly on truth? Fairness requires that I point out that the one time they refer to me—indirectly, of course, because they have never read anything I have written—they inexplicably treat me (relatively speaking) with less venom than they do a multitude of others at whom they take aim. Never have I read a publication containing so much vitriol, such superficiality, so much nonsense, such an allergy to reading, so devoid of the rules of evidence and logic. It reminded me of the infamous Protocols of the Elders of Zion, except that was a forgery and this is the "real thing."

So how do you deal with a group like CWOA when at public forums about schools they present their views? My answer, again, is twofold. Consistent with the political principle they deserve a respectful hearing and a serious, informed response, by which I mean that you should be able to point out that what they advocate were long features of our schools; that sea-swell changes in our society required changes in our schools; that these changes were sin-

cere efforts to deal with new problems; that if these efforts were inef-
fective, it requires new efforts that are not ahistorical repetitions of
past ones; that schools do not "make" society but are "made" by it;
that our schools serve diverse constituencies and the most we can
ask of schools is that they determine and help forge (not unilaterally) a consensus of what is and should be the school program. The
second part of my answer (again) is indirect; that is, unless you have
sincerely involved parents and others so that they understand the
diversity of school problems, the intractability of those problems to
past efforts to ameliorate them, and gain support for mutually
agreed-upon new directions, it becomes an instance of you, and
only you, versus the likes of a CWOA who are literally ignorant of
history, impervious to reason and compromise, and whose intolerance of competing views is exceeded only by a capacity to see con-
spiracy everywhere, not only among educators but among all those
groups seeking to come to grips with an obviously changed and
changing social world.

To my knowledge there is one recommendation in the report of
the Connecticut Commission I have not seen in similar reports: colleges of education should develop courses to help educators develop
"skills" in relating to parents and others. In all of my books on education I have somewhat monotonously pointed out that there is one
function a teacher is expected to and does perform for which he or
she gets absolutely no preparation: how do you talk to and relate to
parents? That omission could be justified only on the basis that
teachers were born with the appropriate genes for such a task or
that it simply was not all that important a task. The first assumption
is, of course, nonsense, and the self-defeating aspects of the second
one today all too apparent. But at the same time I respond with surprise and favor at the Commission's recommendation, I am bothered
by the concept of "skills," which, to me, connotes a technical proficiency devoid of moral, political, historical considerations (e.g., a
skilled carpenter, electrician, surgeon, dentist, radiologist, short-order
cook). From my perspective there are several basic issues about which

educators need a solid education—not training in the sense of train-ing animals but of education as much to flush out, to expose, over-learned attitudes derived from many sources and experience as to make acquisition of new stances possible. What is involved here are two processes: unlearning and learning. (It was the failure to deal with the stresses of unlearning that largely explains why in the six-ties the new math and other new curricula were such disasters for teachers and students. I sat in on a number of summer workshops intended for teachers who would become "skilled" in the new cur-ricula where the teachers of teachers were egregiously insensitive to the stresses that unlearning "old ways" inevitably engenders. To rivet on learning and to ignore unlearning is a prescription for failure or, just as bad, a going-through-the-motions of a superficially acquired skill.)

In regard to parent-community involvement there are questions with which educators would have to come to grips, questions prior to acquisition of "skill":

1. How and why does socialization into a profession create a gulf between the professional and those he or she serves or is ulti-mately responsible to?

2. More specifically, how did the education profession contribute to a situation in which the public today views educators with diminishing respect, trust, and competence?

3. How should one regard the political principle? What are its justifications and why has it been so hard in the past to act consistently and sincerely on it?

4. Why have educators done such a poor job in helping parents and others gain a more sophisticated comprehension of the problems and issues educators grapple with?

5. By what rationale can one conclude that parents and others potentially possess assets that can contribute to substantive-policy issues such as school organization and structure, cur-riculum, hiring, and school-system relationships?

6. What are or will be the *predictable* problems that parents and educators will encounter in forging relationships of mutual trust and respect? Why are they predictable? Why are altered power relationships always problem producing?

7. Why should parents be as accountable for educational outcomes as educators? What are the obvious dangers when only educators are accountable?

8. What should educators know, other than superficially, about the community their school is in, for example, its demographic, religious, economic, vocational, cultural characteristics? Can schools continue to be encapsulated buildings containing encapsulated classrooms walled off from the realities of their communities?

These are a sample of political-moral-educational questions that have to be discussed, digested, and answered prior to "how to do it" questions. There is no one way "to do it"; no one way to structure involvement; no one way that is free of problems; no one way that is not taxing of patience, conflict, and time; and no one way that guarantees productive outcomes. And there is no one way of "doing it" that does not involve the *Sturm und Drang* of the concomitant processes of unlearning and learning. Without learning "how to think it" and "why one should believe it," the doing of it can be a mindless affair.

Chapter Seven

Changing the System

Boards of education, elected or appointed, represent the community, and represent means taking the community's interests, attitudes, and desires into account; insuring that state rules and regulations are met; developing, approving, and defending the school system's budget; approving policies that will sustain or improve educational practice and outcomes. Even though these boards oversee schools that are creations and instruments of state government, they nevertheless potentially have powers to change schools in myriads of ways.[1] Hiring and firing, approving or rejecting a curriculum, setting salary schedules, the construction or renovation of schools—these are only a few of the ways the policies and decisions of boards impact on schools. Members of the board are involved in schools in order to represent and protect the welfare of the community. A board member may or may not have (or had) a child in the public schools; a board member may or may not have any experiential credentials in regard to a school or school system. What a board is expected to possess is the time, energy, motivation, and maturity dispassionately to learn what schools are about and

---

[1] When I use the term *governance structure*, I mean not only boards of education but the state department of education as well. The two, of course, are in relation to each other and very frequently in ways that make innovation and school change difficult, aside from ensuring that the paper manufacturers will show a handsome profit. Although there is a literature on boards of education, there is hardly one on state departments of education, a fact I find puzzling, as if their role is of no practical significance, a conclusion that no member of a state department would think of accepting. As presently constituted, boards and state departments of education are part of the problem and not of the solution.

why, and to use that learning to maintain and improve schools in ways satisfying to the community. A board member is expected to be involved, to be active, to become knowledgeable, to be the opposite of passive in representing the interests of the community and the needs of students. To be elected or to accept appointment to a board of education signifies that the person has the qualities and ability to learn the game and the score.

I had trouble writing that paragraph because so much of it is myth; where it is not myth it is misleading, and where it is not misleading it is of trivial significance about matters I have been discussing. It will not be regarded, I hope, by the reader as a digression if I describe an experience from which I drew "lessons" about boards, any board, responsible for a public agency. It was a lesson I learned in the years 1942–45, and nothing in my subsequent experience disconfirmed its validity.

Up until 1941 Connecticut had one residential "training school" for mentally retarded individuals. In the 1930s the governor appointed a commission to plan and build a second one in the southern part of the state. That commission became the board of trustees. I took my first professional job there a few months after the Southbury Training School opened in the fall of 1941. The board was composed of corporate executives, a professor of pediatrics, a sociologist knowledgeable about the field, and a politically connected parent of a retarded child. Early on in their deliberations and travels around the country the board made a momentous decision. Unlike all the "warehouses" they had seen, the new institution had to be dramatically different in three respects:

1. There would be no large, congregate buildings. There would be cottages with no more than twenty to thirty residents. Each cottage would have its own "mother and father," cook, and kitchen.

2. Southbury was to be an *educational* institution, not a medically dominated one as was then the universal practice.

3. Southbury would have a "revolving door" policy that meant that those who entered would leave after their training was complete. Unlike all other institutions where a resident would be kept for many years, the revolving door rationale would prevent such long stays and the warehousing that was a consequence.

It is no exaggeration to say that the commission-board had identified most of the seamy features of public institutions that decades later led to the deinstitutionalization movement. Nor is it an exaggeration to say that in terms of architecture, educational rationale, and aesthetics Southbury was revolutionary. So why, after a few years, did Southbury go downhill and ultimately end up under the jurisdiction of the courts? The answer is a *very* complicated one, and what follows is a part of it, and in my opinion an important part.

1. In terms of individual life accomplishments, and the courage to depart from tradition, the board came close to being unique. But the board was blatantly unrepresentative of the population of families it was intended to serve, a population very heterogeneous on a variety of factors. There was no sampling of that population to determine why families would or would not seek to institutionalize their children, what their expectations of Southbury were, what knowledge they wanted to acquire to make a decision, and what help they would need to make institutionalization unnecessary. The board proceeded in a noblesse oblige fashion; that is, they, the state, and advisors knew what was best for these families. "Send us your children, and when we return them in not too long a time to you and the community, you will be appreciative"—that was the unverbalized stance.

2. Southbury was built in the middle of rural nowhere. There was no public transportation, the population centers from which it would draw were not around the corner, and those were days when car ownership was far less than today. Given the revolving

door policy, the goal of returning children to home and community, and the board's knowledge that these kinds of institutions had been deliberately placed where they were on an "out of sight, out of mind" attitude, why did they consent to build Southbury where they did? The general answer is that they had no comprehension of the different ways families were affected by and came to regard their retarded child, and how those ways might or might not run counter to the revolving door policy, especially when distance enters the picture. The specific answer is that children and families were abstractions or categories to them that effectively masked the variations they contained. Southbury was planned for categories of people, not for "real" children or families.

3. In choosing a superintendent and department heads the board did not use as a litmus test how well they understood Southbury's rationale and mission, how willing and able they would be to depart from conventional practice. They chose a superintendent who knew next to nothing about mental retardation, a remarkable man for whom appearances were more important than substance, a man who could sell the Brooklyn Bridge several times a day. And he, with board approval, chose a staff from which, among their virtues (and they did not lack virtues), a sense of unconventional mission was absent. But once you went below department heads, virtues were hard to find, let alone a sense of mission. And at the bottom of the hierarchy (attendants, cottage parents) you found very nice people (for the most part) who had no conception whatever of mission, training, and educational policy.

4. The board never understood how complicated life in a complex organization can be for everyone in it, especially when everyone in it *has* to live and work there because of where it has been placed. Smooth and productive social and work relationships anywhere are not all that frequent; in total institutions like Southbury they are predictably infrequent, to indulge understatement. The culture of these institutions—their administrative, top-down structure; the lack of any in-service programs; the lack of forums for

expression of opinions; the division between "the outside and the inside" world; the emphasis on law, order, and regulations—is self-defeating of the experience of growth in everyone. No less than the children for whom they are responsible, the staff cannot resist the pressures to conform, to become passive and resigned in regard to the present and future.

5. Up until Southbury opened, the board gave whatever time and energy were required in the planning and construction process. From the day it opened the board was, for all practical purposes, never on the scene, except for its monthly, brief meetings. In effect, it was as if they had said, "We have planned and created Southbury. From this point on, it is the responsibility of the superintendent and staff to carry out what we started." In fact, when in their infrequent interaction with staff someone tried to discuss problems the institution was encountering, board members made it clear that they had no intention "to intrude" into internal affairs.

It took me at least two years to recognize that Southbury was well on its way to becoming the kind of institution it was intended to supplant. As I said earlier, the full explanation is far more complex than I have indicated, and in focussing on the board, it is no way to suggest that their errors of omission and commission were decisive for what happened to their vision for Southbury. What I related was a way of making several points that characterize almost every board of education with which I have had experience.

The first point is that ignorance of the substance of the arena of problems for which a board member has responsibility may not be lethal but it is certainly not inherently virtuous. It could be argued that such a board member has less to *unlearn*. If you so argue, you are suggesting that it is the responsibility of that person to *learn* what is going on and why, and, I assume, by learning you mean active learning: making and exploiting opportunities to gain first-hand knowledge of how life is perceived and experienced by all groups in the school. That kind of learning is not "intrusive" as long as several criteria are met: that kind of learning is acknowledged as a responsibility of the board member; it is not for the purpose of on-the-spot decision making; whatever information is obtained is inevitably incomplete or misinterpretable in some way and, therefore, has to be judged by other sources of information presented and discussed in other forums; the board member is an openly acknowledged sounding board, not conducting a witch hunt, not undercutting the day-to-day responsibility and authority of others; the board member is in a listening, learning, question-asking role. However you state the criteria, they should reflect the board member's responsibility to the community to have a feel for "what is going on," a basis for raising questions and ultimately for voting on policy issues. I am quite aware that this responsibility is an onerous one requiring time and tact, and not one that is free of problems, but let us not forget that board members are not elected or appointed to be as ignorant of what is going on at the end of their term as they were at the beginning, to cast their votes on the basis of what other people say, not on any direct experience.

In my experience I have never known a board member, however bright, motivated, and well intentioned, who sought actively truly to acquire knowledge about the substance of the important educational issues. And by important I mean organizational climate, job satisfaction of staff, *chronic* problems, classroom atmospheres, and the quality and level of student interest, motivation, activity, and curiosity, to name but a few of the factors that determine educational outcomes. How can a board member vote on anything that affects schools without *some* firsthand experience *in* schools with the different groups upon whom that vote impacts? Apparently, they can and do. In the Southbury anecdote I said that from the time the institution opened the board was rarely on the scene; they literally knew nothing about anything that was going on. Worse yet, they really did not want to know or hear anything that did not come to them "through channels," and that meant the superintendent. In my experience, that is also the case with boards of education.

What board members know or learn is what superintendents (and some of their assistants) want them to learn and know. I do not say that with malice or as an accusation of insincerity. The superintendents are agents of their boards, but it is not infrequent that, psychologically speaking, superintendents regard the boards as *their* agent, in which case the board is getting a particular view of issues and problems. That is not inherently bad as long as it is recognized that it is a particular view that may or may not be justified, in whole or in part. What boards do not confront is that the superintendent and his or her top administrative staff have one thing in common with the board: *what they say are the realities of the school system is not based on firsthand experience in schools; what boards and superintendents know and learn are derived from reports or other forms of communication from lower-level administrators where direct experience in schools is frequently minuscule.* I am reminded here of the game in which elementary school teachers engage their students. The teacher whispers a sentence or so to a student who then has to whisper it to another, and on and on to the last student who then says aloud what was whispered to him or her. The similarity of the teacher's message to what the last child said aloud is either slight or nonexistent. I have sat in on enough meetings of boards of education (and other types of boards) to conclude that it is by no means infrequent for boards and superintendents to discuss policies and actions on the basis of "data" for which the adjectives *valid, objective,* and *clear* are utterly inappropriate; they would be inadmissible in any court of evidence.

Several objections will be raised to what I have said. The first is the "intrusive" or "meddling" argument: to encourage board members to gain direct experiences in schools and classrooms can only undercut the authority and responsibility of administrators and teachers alike, and this by a group with no credentials for comprehending educational issues. This argument is in principle identical to that against parent involvement in decision making, although this objection overlooks the fact that boards are *legally* empowered and morally obligated to be *involved*, to know what is going on, to seek understanding, to be proactive and not passively reactive, to be other than a rubber stamp, an ignorant voter. In its most blatant form it is an argument that education is too important and complex an affair to let nonprofessionals meaningfully enter the scene. If these kinds of arguments overlook the legal and moral responsibilities of boards, they also deny that educators have contributed anything to the inadequacies of our schools, inadequacies that only educators presumably can correct. That denial is not only wrong, it is inexcusable. There is a saying that "war is too important to be left to the generals," and that is true for education, medicine, law, and more.

A second argument is one I have gotten from board members with whom I have discussed these issues. It goes like this: "You seem to be vastly underestimating how much time we have to spend in reading reports on all kinds of matters, committee meetings of one kind or another, the regular board meeting that can go on for hours and that averages more than one a month, interviewing candidates for top positions, and then there are budgetary issues and the preparation of the budget that involve mind-boggling details like should we repair this school rather than that school. And if there is a new school to be built, or one that should be closed, or it is a year in which new union contracts have to be negotiated, there go our evenings and even some of our days. Most board members have jobs—they also have families—and there is only a limited amount of time you can expect a board member to give, which is why some of them don't want another term. They paid their dues. We have no alternative to depending on the superintendent and his staff to provide us with the information we need. Even if the criticisms you are making have merit, and I don't think they do, they are unreasonable and unrealistic." I shall return to this argument later.

The third argument is an implicit one in that it accepts the traditional board-administrative-school structure and relationships but explains the plethora of problems by the deficiencies of people, be they on the board, in administrative positions, or in the classroom, or in political positions outside of the school system. Change people and you will desirably change schools. Employ better personnel selection procedures, develop better and more stringent criteria for job performance, mandate more continuing education credits, make it less a life career to fire an inadequate but tenured teacher, improve the quality of preparatory programs for educators, and choose board members who have independent minds and are not beholden to or captives of political figures or a racial or religious group or a "one agenda" group. It is hard to quarrel with any of these suggestions. Alone or in combination these suggestions completely bypass the problem of how the present structure and its undergirding rationale, indeed its ideology about relationships within and among different groups in the hierarchy, set drastic limits on the consequences of "people" changers. More specifically, the structure and rationale have given us a school culture devoid of forums that serve the purpose of ensuring that the ideas, attitudes, and proposals of the different groups can be voiced and discussed instead of going underground (or nowhere) or being, as it now is, a limitless supply of fodder for a rumor mill. Structures do have rationales, and in the case of our schools it is a rationale that guarantees that each layer of the hierarchy will have a distorted conception of adjacent layers. The lines between them are literally drawn, and there are no forums (call them what you will) for a meaningful exchange. And a meaningful exchange has to meet three criteria: it does not inhibit expression of strong differences in views; the right of participants to represent their views is an acknowledged political right; there are no penalties for expressing views. I can assure the reader that I know that those are criteria for "ideal" exchanges, which in this world we can only approximate. But approximations are better than having no forums at all, and they are better than token gestures recognized privately as such by everyone. I am describing forums that are developed precisely and deliberately as recognition that the existing structure gives rise to problems far more than it resolves them.

Boards of education do not serve the function of a forum, and their encapsulated, elevated status—like their counterparts on top of the mountain in Kafka's castle—renders them insensitive to the degree to which the basis on which they make decisions is incomplete, distorted, and slanted, because the structure and rationale of the system violates the spirit of the political principle. *So, as I have emphasized in previous chapters, just as parent-community involvement is justified by the political principle, that principle is no less justified in regard to relationships among the different groups in the school system.* Boards of education operate on the myth that they understand the system for which they are responsible. Someone once said that boards see only the tips of icebergs. A listener disagreed and said, "Yes, they deal with tips, but they don't know there is an iceberg underneath."

Boards of education are an anachronism with an ancestry going back to the one-room schoolhouse. Whatever virtues they may have had no longer are evident or even possible. They are now part of the problem, not of the solution. That is a conclusion that many people, in and out of schools, have voiced in the post–World War II era. Martin and Harrison (1972) have written a very interesting book, *Free to Learn*. Far from singling out or scapegoating boards of education for the ills of our schools, these authors present a thought-provoking rationale for a thorough-going alteration of educational governance regardless of where in the community educational needs are expressed. The following excerpt gives the reader a glimpse of the kinds of changes Martin and Harrison recommend:

> Society has a mind-set that the size of school boards was for all time established as a number between five and twelve. It is as though society were trapped into accepting the problem with built-in absolutes it couldn't change. The old trick of connecting nine dots on a sheet of paper with just three straight lines is insoluble if our minds accept the assumption that the lines cannot extend out onto the paper beyond the dots. Once that assumption is disposed of, with the recognition that it is self-imposed, the solution to the problem is evi-

dent. If we discard the self-imposed assumption that to get greater representation we need to repeat the pattern of the small, colonial school committee, the direction toward the answer becomes clear. The answer is to form a new body of greater size, to establish voting districts for education across the face of a city or school district, and to send representatives to the new governing body.

We call this new body an Education Assembly. It would be large, but it would not be elected at large. And its size would serve to promise its performance as a legislative body, while tending to reduce the propensity to become its own executive agent again.

The new body would be designed to perform better four major tasks necessary to improve education. First, it would provide for greater representation. Second, the assembly would be internally organized to function as a legislative body with the necessary structure and staff to perform that role efficiently. Third, the assembly would hold the executive agency accountable for the effectiveness with which programs are carried out. And fourth, the assembly, freed from administrative chores and operational responsibilities, would be able to examine alternative ways of reaching educational objectives in addition to or instead of present school forms. . . .

The Education Assembly would be organized into standing and ad hoc committees which would conduct hearings to determine the community's needs; take expert testimony; publish staff reports detailing alternative ways of reaching an educational goal; analyze the merits, demerits, and costs of each of the alternatives; and convert best judgment into appropriate legislation.

As standard procedure, all legislation establishing new programs would require a preliminary evaluation of the new programs within ninety days of inauguration, and an annual audit. The assembly would establish a program evaluation agency to serve it for this purpose. In areas of major change, where an additional review is desired, the Education Assembly should contract for intensive appraisal and audit by an outside agency. All reviews and reports upon completion would be made public.

The Education Assembly would establish a governing board for each agency and institution it authorizes. These local boards would be elected by residents of the area and by the people served. The board would be the local community's representatives holding agencies accountable for the roles set by the assembly's legislation and keeping them close to the people served.

The Education Assembly would work with other agencies of government. One of the weaknesses of our present processes is the isolation of the schools and their boards of education from the other operations of local government. This isolation was engendered and maintained because of the fear that politics and the schools would mix at the cost of good education. Unfortunately, the price paid for immunity to political patronage and party pressures has been fragmented health programs and limited resources being wasted on duplicate and overlapping programs. School playing fields unrelated to and unused by municipal recreation activities, plans for mass housing units that ignore educational needs, and highways and other transportation routes changed without reference to the plans of boards of education have been unhappy commonplaces.

There are towns, communities, and neighborhoods where planning for education is considered too important to involve the local board of education. There is scarcely a municipality where the neglect of educational needs while preparing the master plan isn't due in large measure to the traditional aloofness displayed by boards of education toward other branches of government.

Our Education Assembly would be involved.

Involved because education receives most of the local tax revenue and is a major user of land, and because those who are responsible for educational planning must be vitally concerned with health services, recreation, transportation, the arts, museums, libraries, theaters, and the general life of the community.

The Education Assembly would move from the fiction of non-involvement to the reality of direct cooperation with other agencies in planning total service to the community. And the Education Assembly as a new legislative arm of state government would have the power to tax and borrow money for the purposes of education.

It is hoped that many of the restraints now imposed on boards of education by state governments, such as those limiting tax rates and requiring more than a simple majority to pass a referendum, would be relaxed because these restrictions are historically related to education's political isolation and the need to restrain local boards of education.

Because institutional form tends to control institutional functions, we strongly advocate the abolition of school committees and boards of education that are anachronistic forms in twentieth century urban America.

In their place we urge a new legislative body that is . . .

• broadly representative.

• organized to determine the desires and needs of a community for better education.

• free of the old assumption that schools are the only places where learning can take place.

• free of the old assumption that children are education's only clients.

• free of the old assumption that the concerns of other governmental agencies are not also its concerns.

• required by design to hold administrators accountable. No longer would a board of education turn to its executive arm for an accounting only to say in bewilderment, "We have met the administrator, and he is us."

• required by design to measure and evaluate the performance of each agency it creates.

This new legislative body—the Education Assembly—is the first of our new forms for education. It is long overdue for American education [pp. 37–42].

Among the suggested offshoots of the Education Assembly are a Community Arts Center, a Career Education Center, a Community

Guidance and Evaluation Center, Mini Schools, Adult Neighborhood Centers, and Children's Neighborhood Learning Centers. There are three refreshing assumptions underlying Martin and Harrison's suggestions. First, the political principle informs every one of their suggestions, *and that includes the contexts in which children learn.* Second, education should not take place only in classrooms in schools; in any community there are adults who need and desire an educational experience relevant to their interests. Third, no program should be approved, or initiated, or maintained unless it has been scrutinized and evaluated by several sources, including ones that are independent and hired specifically for each program. Fourth, any effort to reform the structure of governance of education, broadly conceived, that essentially leaves the existing structure intact is a waste of time, money, and energy (i.e., a doomed affair). That is a prediction that has been totally, devastatingly confirmed in the years since that book was written in 1972, and which explains why in 1990 I wrote *The Predictable Failure of Educational Reform.* Indeed, since 1972 (and before) there has been a number of educators, notably John Goodlad and Larry Cuban, who have pointed out, in my opinion conclusively, that although issues of governance are crucial, so is a very long overhaul of preparatory programs for educators, which is why in 1993 I wrote *The Case for Change: Rethinking the Preparation of Educators.* In *Educational Renewal* Goodlad (1994) continues to be "cautiously optimistic" and hopes that I am too, despite the fact that both of us know what we are up against. Well, as long as John Goodlad continues his action programs and writings I am not completely devoid of hope. But I am reminded here of the optimist who said, "This is the best of all possible worlds," and the pessimist who replied, "I am afraid you are right."

I did not direct attention to the Martin and Harrison book as a way of saying that I think we ought to accept their rationale for altered governance of education. I completely agree with their call for the elimination of boards of education, and I applaud their seriousness and sincerity in invoking the political principle, and I find their suggestions for what altered governance might look like thought-provoking. I assume that they, like me, hear, when we hear at all, from the converted: those who already have come to similar conclusions and write to tell us that they now feel less alone. However, our purpose is not to dispense supportive psychotherapy, certainly not a central purpose! What the Martin and Harrison book did for me was to give greater force to questions about which I obsess, ones that are implicit but undiscussed by them. Is it realistic to expect that required alterations in the governance of education can come from *within* the educational communities, local and state? In one brief paragraph (p. 41) in their book they acknowledge in passing that their suggestions would be possible only if there was enabling state legislation. But how can a state legislature pass legislation about problems of which they are ignorant or about which they know only what the state board of education has told them, a board that, like the local boards, is not about to look favorably on any radical change in governance? And, I need hardly add, one should not expect that state associations of school administrators will endorse any proposal that they see as undercutting their status and power. And teacher associations and unions, however militant they have been about salary scales and conditions of work, have steered clear of the issues we have been discussing, even though many of their leaders and members will privately condemn the existing structure, at the same time they are in a symbiotic relationship with boards of education. (I have learned enough about union-board collective bargaining sessions and relationships not to expect that we can rely on unions to advocate, at the least, the elimination of boards of education.) Unfortunately, there is nothing said by the national leadership of the two teacher unions to allow one to be hopeful that they will use their roles to call for changes in school governance.

I read Albert Shanker's column in the Sunday *New York Times* religiously because, more often than not, he at least writes about important issues. As I read him *between the lines*, Shanker knows full well that drastic changes in the structure of governance are necessary if the downhill slide in the quality of education is to be stopped, let alone improved. For example, in one of his columns Shanker (1994) begins by discussing some suggestions made by Mark Freedman's (1993) *The Kindness of Strangers: Adult Mentors, Urban Youth and the New Voluntarism*. In the second half of the column Shanker says:

Freedman's suggestion is that we look at existing institutions, like schools, where possibilities for mentoring arise naturally. Teachers and other school personnel don't have to be parachuted into students' lives; they know these kids and work with them every day. And the personal concern mentors feel for the youngsters they work with is a natural extension of the teacher-pupil relationship rather than the kindness of a stranger, which must often seem rather artificial.

The problem is that schools are not *organized* in a way that gives teachers and students a chance to develop close and caring relationships—and they don't have the resources to do it either. Elementary school children spend one year with a teacher—just long enough to *start* feeling comfortable—and then they move on to a new teacher. After elementary school, they often have a different teacher for each subject.

Why shouldn't elementary and junior high school students stay with the same group of kids for three or four years? Why shouldn't there be a team of teachers and paraprofessionals, and why shouldn't the class be broken down into small groups so each group can work closely with a teacher—and get to know one another? In high school, mentoring could be carried on by programming small weekly seminars, which would continue—same teacher and same kids—throughout the students' high school years. Or all these changes could be carried out in smaller schools or schools within schools, where students and teachers start out with a better chance of knowing one another.

These ideas are sound in educational as well as emotional and moral terms. Students who are connected with another adult, and with one another, are less likely to drop out. And they are more likely to work and shape one another up—and thus to enjoy a measure of success in school work.

Mentoring can fill an important need for the many youngsters who have no close or caring relationship with an adult. But we are kidding ourselves if we think we can make a dent in this enormous problem with ad-hoc arrangements. We should stop working around the edges of the main institution concerned with children—the schools—and concentrate on making our schools moral communities. It can be done.

The italics for the word *organized* are mine. That word plus the contents of what I quoted justify the conclusion—and I do not think I am putting words in his mouth—that Shanker knows full well that the ways schools and school systems are organized and governed are inimical to innovation and meaningful change; that is, they are governed and run to continue as they are, a tinkering here and a tinkering there, a cosmetic change here and a cosmetic change there. Shanker knows the game and the score (I do not always agree with him on the score), but, however forthright he has been on most matters, he has been silent on the governance issue. In a column several years ago he courageously asked, Can teacher unions any longer avoid taking a stance on the most important issues of educational policy, to break out of the labor union tradition of not intruding into the prerogatives of management? He knew then as he does now what the answer should be, but, unfortunately, he has been silent. He is but one of the knowledgeable people in and out of the educational arena who has avoided confronting openly the stultifying consequences of educational governance. I can assure the reader that when I say many I know whereof I speak. What I have said in these pages I did not dream up, nor does it mean that these people had ready answers or were in full agreement. What it does mean is that in regard to governance there are many people who have made the correct diagnosis, wrapped up in the observation that not only is the parading emperor naked but he has a terminal disease.

And what about our universities, colleges of education, and the scores of educational associations concerned with research, policy, practice, and school governance? Here again there is a gulf between what people publicly say and write and what they will say privately. Almost without exception what they publicly propose assumes that the existing governance structure will and should continue. What they say privately stamps them as the optimist-pessimist I noted earlier.

Let me rephrase the question. What needs to happen for altered school governance to become a legislative concern (and by that I mean more than parent-community involvement)? The answer to that question is contained in the answer to this question: What is likely to happen if the issues surrounding school governance do not gain currency? My answer is that slowly but surely the public schools will get worse, alternative forms of schooling will become available to parents, our urban schools will become day care centers (at best) containing untoward social dynamics (at worst), and because of public dissatisfaction monetary support for the schools will shrink. Put in another way, *I am predicting a continuation of what has already happened and is happening.* Those predictions require no special knowledge except knowledge of what has happened, of the *intractability* of schools to change despite sincere efforts and the expenditure of scores of billions of dollars. I cannot predict when it will happen but at some point legislatures and the public, having been hit over the head by an obvious social catastrophe with percolating effects throughout the society, will confront the issues of governance, the worst possible context for dispassionate, reasoned discussion and action.

More out of desperation than inspiration, I wrote *Letters to a Serious Education President* (Sarason, 1993b). One of the major themes was that nothing, but nothing, would be accomplished in school reform unless and until the president, with congressional support, convened a convention or commission specifically to consider, among other things, alternatives to present forms of school governance. Education today, I said, was similar to (really worse than) the situation the American states were in under the Articles of Confederation. That is, there was clear evidence that the Articles were no basis for forging and sustaining a nation. That is why in 1787 there was a constitutional convention to come up with a new basis that was more likely to keep the colonies together. The important, indeed crucial, point was that *everyone* at that convention agreed on one point: the Articles of Confederation were inadequate and dangerous in regard to preserving the goals of the revolution. Initially, at least, they differed widely among themselves about the substance of change, and it was not until three months of the most sustained, amazingly candid, searching, comprehensive discussion in human history, that they came up with a document they could present to the states for ratification, which was gained only after there was agreement about adding a Bill of Rights. I told the president that in regard to protecting the existence of our public schools only he could tell the nation why he was appointing a commission to address the problem of governance (among other things), and to address meant to confront the fact that the existing form of governance could no longer remain as it is, that many people in and outside of the educational community had lost confidence in the governance structure; too much was at stake to permit the issues to remain off the nation's agenda; he was not elected president to preside over the deterioration of the public schools.

What I did not, and should have, told the president is that the participants in the 1787 convention did not have or need a staff of experts to tell them what the problems were. They knew what the problems were even if they disagreed on how to remedy them. We all know about "commissions" composed of well-known, well-placed, well-intentioned people whose main function is to put their imprimatur on information and reports provided them by staff "experts" not noted for their vision, courage, and firsthand knowledge of what schools are, individuals quite adept at coming up with clichés, ear-catching phrases, generalizations, and abstractions that sound wise and sober but are devoid of concrete meaning and direction. We need another commission like that like we need a hole in our collective head. A commission needs a staff, but what it needs more are some members with demonstrated interest and experience in school governance, some who are not educators but have a track record in regard to organizational theory, research, *and* practice, and some legislators who have devoted themselves to reform of school governance. All that I am suggesting here is that the choice of commission members not be determined by the need to "window-dress." It should be a heterogeneous group homogeneous in one respect: they already know that governance of education is in need of drastic reform, not tinkering. It should be a commission very self-conscious of its responsibility (as were those at the 1787 constitutional convention) to come up with a blueprint and a rationale for a new structure for school governance. What they will give us will not have the force of law, national, state, or local. (It is safe to assume that there would be minority reports or appendixes.) But, given the fact that the commission will have been created by the president, one would hope with congressional approval, *it will serve the overarching purpose of giving currency to issues that demand far more public scrutiny and discussion than they have heretofore received.* And, if I and others are right, the citizenry in general, and many educators in particular, are ready to hear what such a commission might propose. It will not come as a bombshell but will be greeted with relief that at long last we are getting to where a major problem is.

In the 1930s President Roosevelt wanted to propose universal health coverage but was dissuaded from doing so because the controversy it would engender would endanger passage of the Social Security Act. When President Truman did make such a proposal, he was regarded as a visionary or a subversive socialist. When that same issue came to the fore in President Johnson's administration in connection with the Medicare act, all kinds of vested interests made short shrift of it. And, yet, during all of these decades the majority of people knew that there was something fundamentally wrong and unjust about a so-called health *system* in which quality care, however defined, was available only to those who could afford it. The medical, pharmaceutical, and business communities—as well as those wedded to certain political ideologies—successfully fought against the principle of universal health insurance. They knew what they were against; they did not know what they were for that stood a chance of dealing with the problem. That there was a problem no one denied, but it was always put on the back burner as if somehow it would not have to be directly confronted. But the problem did not go away; it got worse. So, when President Clinton in 1993 appeared before the Congress and insisted on the acceptance of the principle of universal coverage, the positive response was unanimous; changing the health system could not be postponed. The principle is not in question, the debate about how to act on that principle has begun, and it is quite a debate, as it should be. But that debate would not be possible had the president not stated that the problem could no longer be ignored, no ifs, ands, or buts. And a receptive citizenry responded as if to say, "Finally, we are facing reality."

So why did I write *Letters to a Serious Educational President?* First, the status of our schools is a national concern; it would not be an exaggeration to say national anxiety. No one denies that there is a problem; few can comprehend why past efforts to deal with it have been feckless. Second, just as there has been and is a smoldering resentment toward medical and allied communities, there is no less resentment toward educators and their "bureaucracies." Third, the educational community has provided no leadership in regard to school governance, even though many within it know that issues of governance should not be on the back burner, that although there are other important issues, they are not likely to be dealt with in any semblance of adequacy *independent of an altered school governance*. Fourth, it is only a president serious and courageous enough to say to the congress and the public, "Finally, we must face reality," who can justify to me that I should feel, as John Goodlad does, "cautiously optimistic."

·   Earlier I asked, What is likely to happen if issues surrounding governance do not gain currency? The day after I wrote those words there appeared on the first page of the *New York Times* an article with the heading "Private Groups to Run 15 Schools in Experiment by Massachusetts." Here are its opening paragraphs:

> In the nation's widest experiment in letting private groups run alternative public schools, Massachusetts today turned over 15 schools to private management, including the first schools to be run by the for-profit Edison Project.
>
> In naming 13 different organizations to run the new schools, which will be designed from scratch, the state will have an unusual ability to compare the results of various reform strategies. Edison, for instance, will introduce a longer school year of 210 days, 30 more than the state requires.
>
> A group led by a retired rear admiral will open a boarding school for homeless children that emphasizes technical training. The Cape Cod National Seashore and several Cape Cod cultural organizations will open an "educational village" at Brewster.
>
> The organizations include teachers' collectives, private community organizations, colleges and nonprofit foundations, as well as the Whittle Corporation, which owns Project Edison. Their new public schools share several common elements of school reform, stressing smaller classes, emphasizing basics and teaching about morality and ethics while following state curriculum guidelines.
>
> Seven other states have these so-called "charter" schools, and 10 more have considered them or are considering the schools that essentially bypass local school bureaucracy and many state regulations and report directly to state authorities. They are thus allowed

much greater latitude than traditional schools in hiring and dismissing personnel, purchasing and budgeting, and scheduling.

California began its experiment two years ago, setting a limit of 100 schools in private management. But no other state has issued so many charters at once to such a disparate group of organizations.

It is not my purpose here to prejudge how these schools will fare. It is my purpose to emphasize that the article is certainly evidence of three things: recognition on the part of some state officials that existing governance of our schools—indeed, *of school systems and state departments of education*—is a roadblock to reform; this recognition is fueled by an iceberg of resentment and desperation of which we are seeing only the tips; and the leadership of this movement (and it has the characteristics of a movement, a beginning coalescing of heretofore unrelated individuals and actions) comes primarily from noneducators (e.g., governors and mayors).

It has long been noted that *national* revolutions (e.g., the American, French, and Russian revolutions of 1917) come about *after* rising expectations are endangered or unfulfilled. Beginning in the 1950s increasing numbers of people saw grounds for expecting that the public schools could be transformed and improved by infusions, by no means minuscule, of money, new educational theories and practices, and the belief that good intentions will have desirable outcomes. If not all desirable outcomes, at least enough to sustain the belief that things were moving in the right direction, not only in this or that isolated school but in schools *generally*. With each passing year evidence to sustain such an expectation could be found only by those who confused hope with evidence and reality. The disillusionment today is all too clear, and we are witness not only to a kind of backlash but to proposals literally revolutionary in intent in that they seek radically to change school governance. Revolutions are about issues of power, its sources, allocations, and uses. Revolutions are uprisings against the way things are. They are rarely univocal in stated goals and means. They are, initially at least, composed of different groups with different agendas, having only in common the aim to demolish an existing form and style of governance, and that may include groups that seek to undo what is in order to bring back what they believe was an earlier state of grace. I am not being dramatic when I say that in regard to school governance the seeds of revolutionary actions are beginning to sprout. When and how they will blossom I cannot predict. But that they will blossom I have absolutely no doubt. I should tell the reader that I do not contemplate such blossoming with enthusiasm, if only because revolutions (save the American one) tend to devour their makers, to confirm the maxim that the more things change the more they remain the same. That is why I plead that *now* is the time for a federal commission whose responsibility is to present us with alternatives (plural) to what we know to be manifestly, and very obviously, inadequate. That commission would have no legislative powers, only the power to put into currency the need for change and the concrete possibilities that merit discussion. There are many people who would like to see the barricades protecting the existing governance structure stormed and demolished. I allow myself to hope and believe, in the spirit of the 1787 constitutional convention, that the changes required can be realized after a debate about issues that have been clearly and reasonably posed. But that cannot happen if the need for changes in school governance remains under and not on the table of discussion.

In the next chapter I turn to an issue intimately related to but not identical with issues of governance. In the 1787 convention the founding fathers were crystal clear about their overarching purpose: to forge and sustain a nation based on clearly stated values and rights about how life should be lived, individually and collectively. They sought a structure of governance that would protect those values and rights. So, in the next chapter I take up the questions, What are the most important values and rights school governance should foster? When push comes to shove, is there *an* overarching purpose that if not met or approximated requires us to say that schooling has failed us? I will concentrate on that overarching purpose. If I single out that purpose in the next chapter, it is because it is one with which every reader will agree, and for the right reasons, even though it is one that our schools have hardly approximated or even respected, not because anyone willed or takes delight in the situation but because unimprisoning ourselves from the burden of theories, practices, and governance structures no longer adequate—features each of us "grew up" with—is the hardest task of all.

Chapter Eight

The Purpose of Schools

Let us start with the first physical-psychological-educational site we "attend," namely the unit we call a family. And let us ask this question: Why do parents have children? The answers are many, ranging from religious reasons to "they just came along." But whatever the reason, once the child is born parents begin to think and fantasize about what that child may, could, might, or should be. Parents, of course, want the child to be healthy and happy, but they also want the child to be a distinctive "something" (e.g., rich businessperson, celebrated actor, great writer, doctor, lawyer, scientist). Parents are used to saying that they want the child to be whatever he or she chooses to be, implying that it is morally wrong to foist their desires and goals on the child. I say "morally wrong" because they are implying that it is an unjust exercise of their powers to mold the child in accordance with parental dreams, that to do so would be a source of guilt. I have never talked with parents who, when pressed, would not admit that they would feel fulfilled if the child became the "something" of their fantasies.

But why fear the guilt, why is it so important that the something a child becomes should come from his or her experience, interests, and talents? Such importance was very rare in earlier centuries, and there are literally billions of parents and children today in different parts of this earth where choosing to be a something does not exist as a problem; survival is the problem. It is a western, especially American, problem. Why this is so, how it came about, is a long, complicated story far beyond the purposes of this book even to sketch. Let me just say that if the something a child is to become or shaped increasingly became *psychologically* an issue for parents, and, therefore, for children over the past couple of centuries, it erupted like a volcano into national consciousness as a consequence of the mammoth upheavals that were consequences of World War II. Few people, if any, were exempt from these consequences. Lives, attitudes, outlooks, time perspectives, definitions of self, identifications with the past—all these and more underwent sea-swell changes. And one of those changes was implied in the very frequent parental declaration, "We made a mess of this world; our children should have the opportunity to shape a better world." And that change was also reflected in the labels applied to the decades after World War II: "The Age of Psychology," "The Age of Mental Health." It was a change about parental responsibility in regard to respecting and reinforcing a child's individuality, expanding and not restricting the child's options for new experience, and fostering independence of, not dependence on, parent dreams. Contained in that change is the answer to my earlier question, But why fear the guilt, why is it so important that the something a child becomes should come up from his or her experience, interests, and talents? There was good reason why Dr. Spock's book about child health and rearing became the bible for millions of parents anxious (not only concerned, but anxious) to know what children are and how one comes to understand where they are psychologically coming from and going, a coming and going that if ignored or misunderstood would have untoward effects.

Someone said that the children born in the "Age of Permissiveness" were those who became the "Me Too" generation. That is an oversimplification and a very misleading one because it completely ignores perhaps the most obvious feature of the post–World War II years. I refer to the fact that as never before children and adults could literally *see* the world and because of speedier modes of transportation (e.g., jets, cross-country interstate highways) could experience it other than vicariously. It was not only that children were taught to expect more and to experience more of this world than had been true for their parents; the expectations of and for children were more possible than ever before in human history. You *could* be what you wanted to be; you *should* be what you want to be; there is a world to conquer, and you should try to conquer it. Those are not new themes in the American psyche, but they mightily increased in strength in the post–World War II era. If for circumstances not of their making many children would not have their expectations realized, they nevertheless heard and absorbed those themes, even those parents who knew that there was a difference between the rhetoric and realities of those expectations.

I started this chapter by asking why parents have children, and I have answered (all too briefly) the question by saying that, however varied the answers, the goal of parents in the post–World War II years was to capitalize on the child's natural curiosity to explore and experience, to want to be competent, to feel their interests have not been ignored.

In the musical *Carousel*, the setting of which is in bygone days in New England, the roguish male central character sings "My Boy Bill," the longest soliloquy in the musical theater. In the first half of the song he expresses in the most macho fashion his expectations-fantasies about the boy he will father, a replica of himself. The music is appropriately stirringly macho. And then he suddenly stops as he realizes that the child he will father may be a girl. He is stunned, but only momentarily. And then to music that is delicate, soft, and poignant he describes his girl as one who will meet all of his conceptions of what a girl should be. Billy Bigelow knew what that child would be, *he* would make sure of that. In recent decades that parental stance is less than rare, replaced by one that (publicly at least) gave top priority to the individuality-uniqueness of the child. Permissiveness conjures up the wrong imagery, as if parents were indiscriminate about the child's interests and desires. It would be more correct to say that parents felt between a rock and a hard place: on the one hand, fearful that they may not be sufficiently aware of or sensitive to or providing sufficient stimulation to the child and, on the other hand, conscious of the importance of not foisting their dreams and hopes on the young child. It is no wonder that parents sought help and reassurance from Dr. Spock and many other Dr. Spocks. The message that parents heard and bought was "you could harm a child by shaping him or her in your image, or you could support a child to find his or her developmental path." And that message did not come only from the Dr. Spocks but also from a body of research indicating that from its earliest days the child is on a developmental course characterized by stages in which cognitive characteristics (e.g., exploration, curiosity, memory, perception) become increasingly differentiated in the context of an emerging picture of self, others, and the surrounding world; and the productive consequences of that development depend on how well parents understood, respected, and supported that complicated development. The child was not passive human clay to be molded in *an* image, waiting, so to speak, to become *a* something in accord with parental dreams. It was an active, purposeful, quizzical, experience devouring, competence-seeking human clay with the potential to become more than the one parentally inspired "image." If any label captures what I have been describing, it is "The Age of the Child-Centered Parent."

The above, I should hasten to add, is intended only to convey the change in many people (by no means all!) in their view of their children and their parental obligations. Historically speaking, it was a momentous change, if only because it recognized to a greater degree than before the importance of taking account of what young, developing children are, psychologically speaking. That is, they literally are not mindless; they come into this world with the potentials derived from a developmental "code," a code that can be blunted or nurtured; they are a complicated something long before they become an adult something. Ignore all that and you have shortchanged the child.

There was a problem, however, a very predictable one that parents encountered: you can read the Spocks of this world, you can articulate and agree with everything they say, you can try to act consistently with what you "know" and "learned," but, as one parent put it, "When I have to deal with *my* unique, *concrete* child in *concrete* situations that are never simple, that do not tell me with textbook clarity what I should do or think, situations not of my making and too frequently not under my control, I often find myself reacting unreflectively, really instinctively, and then I feel guilty that I may have screwed up" (emphasis mine). That is the kind of statement I have heard from eminent colleagues in child development when they describe, both with humor and chagrin, their departures (with their children) from what they believe to be the "right" way of thinking and acting. The real world of children, mothers, fathers, sibs, and a lot more, is not organized to allow consistency between theory and practice to be other than a sometime thing. There were (and still are) parents who pinpointed with guilt to this or that departure that had untoward effects on the child, and that guilt increased for those parents aware that the number of departures were not small in number. Have I been too harsh, too constricting, too insensitive, too permissive, too indulgent, too blind, too inconsistent, too undecisive? These and other questions plagued parents who accepted the responsibility to identify and nurture the individuality of their offspring, to respect that individuality, not to confuse *this* child with the category of "children" in general. No parent operates without some conception of what is good and bad, right or wrong, problem producing or problem avoiding in regard to child rearing. When that conception is based on the belief (which I regard as a fact) that each child is unique in terms of his or her combination of temperament, cognitive characteristics, reactivity, curiosity, interests—a combination we try to signify by the abstraction *personality*—consistency between theory and practice, conception and action, will inevitably fall short of our mark. That is obvious and predictable, and my purpose here is not to labor the obvious but rather to emphasize that in the post–World War II era more people than ever before came to regard it as self-evident what the Spocks of this world were saying: *this* child is like all other children at the same time he or she is different from all other children, and it is the parental responsibility to identify, exploit, and support that individuality in ways that are productive of the potentials that individuality suggests. The emphasis on individuality is not new in American history or psyche, but that emphasis until relatively recently was primarily in regard to adult individuality and adult self-responsibility for accomplishment (i.e., "making something of yourself"). Beginning in the latter part of the nineteenth century, and accelerating in this century, was the view that adult individuality depended on many things, not the least of which was the fostering of that individuality in the preschool years.

That change in emphasis suffused the rhetoric of educators from whom hopeful parents heard that the goal of schooling was to help each child "realize his or her potential." I say rhetoric because the implications of that statement totally ignored the chasm between those implications and the history and structure of the public schools. The Spockian messages were read by parents with one, two, or several children. Schools as they are were developed for classrooms with many more children. In the development of our schools were obvious features that, although many historians have written about, most (otherwise knowledgeable) people have forgotten or never knew:

1. Because of wave after wave of massive immigrations, public schools classrooms contained forty or fifty or more students. The concept or value placed on individuality was not a luxury; it was simply not in the picture.

2. The goal of schooling was not to explore or "get out of" students their individual interests and talents but rather to "put into them" knowledge-facts considered essential to citizenship and work. Students were trained, not educated, they were passive, not active learners; they were judged by how well they could memorize and

recall, not how well they could think for themselves; they were question answerers, not question askers; they were there to be molded regardless of individual variations.

3. Pedagogical theory was concerned with classroom organization, the authoritative and didactic role of the teacher, maintenance of discipline, techniques that made for efficiency of coverage of a totally predetermined curriculum, instilling proper "work or mental skills," and upholding American values. It was pedagogical theory tailor made to teach masses, not individuals. The practical realities determined theory as much as theory determined practice. It was these kinds of theories and practices against which John Dewey rebelled at the end of the nineteenth century. Dewey started with the question, What are the psychological characteristics of the developing child? The conventional theory and practice started with the question, What do *we* want *them* to become? Dewey saw teachers of the time as "commanders," and his use of that word referred to the military-like role of teachers and the soldier-like obedient, conforming obligations of students.

4. The administrative-bureaucratic structure of schools and school systems, the pressures to segregate poor learners, and the initiation of age-graded classes were primary consequences of the attempt to make schools more efficient, in principle similar to the ways in which the manufacturing industries were increasing their productivity and efficiency. When Henry Ford said that you could purchase any color Ford you desired as long as it was black, he was conveying the message that what consumers wanted would not interfere with an efficient mode of production, the products of which were indistinguishable from each other. If you can imagine Ford cars having "minds," you can also imagine how the bulk of students felt, not counting, of course, the large number who dropped out. Dropping out, now and then, included an undetermined number of consumers who wanted to be other than a black Ford. (Not so incidentally, that was and is the case for some students who drop out of college.)

The preceding is by way of description and not criticism. If there is a note of criticism, it refers to the fact that as the decades passed, as the Deweyan perspective gained currency, as researchers demonstrated the individualities and communalities of psychological development, as the clash between the cultural backgrounds of multicultural America became plain to see, and as schools remained monolithically organized and incapable of "flexing" to individual variations—schools remained pretty much as they had been at the same time that the rhetoric of individuality became more shrill. The insights, the evidence, and the rhetoric changed; practice and organization did not. No one denied that "teachers should teach children, not subject matter." That maxim was intended as a criticism of what was obvious in the classroom. Even though today the number of students in a classroom is much less than earlier decades in this century, "teaching students, not subject matter" is the rule, not the exception, despite the fact that, unless my experience is atypical, teachers know in their heart of hearts that neither by their preparation nor by the ways schools are organized can they give other than lip service to individuality. And if the reader has any question about that observation, I hope it does not extend to what to me (and many others) is an indisputable conclusion: the bulk of students experience classrooms as boring, stultifying places where they are compelled to be in order to learn facts for reasons not at all clear to them, not related to their interests and concerns, incomparably less stimulating than the world they see and their experience outside of school.

Let me ask why in the post–World War II era did the public become dissatisfied with our schools? The answer was that test scores steadily decreased. That is like saying that if your child has a high fever and it gets higher, then you should be worried. Decreasing test scores like an increasing high fever tell us we have a problem; they do not tell us what the answer is; they tell us we should seek answers. However unsophisticated we may be about matters of health, we know than an increasing high fever means that something is *systemically* wrong with us (i.e., something is awry with our bodily physiology-chemistry). In the case of decreasing test scores the answers were many, but they did not call into question the system qua system, its usual way of doing and justifying its business, so to speak. That is to say, the system was basically appropriate, and its outcomes would be improved if, for example, curricula were changed, new pedagogical techniques employed, preparing educators more steeped in subject matter, giving more time to the "basics," insisting on and maintaining performance standards students should meet, involving parents more in matters educational, instituting preschool programs that made it more likely that children would be able to benefit more from formal schooling—these and other "answers" had in common the unverbalized acceptance of schools as they have been and are: their governance structure; their decision-making processes; their encapsulated classrooms; their relation to preparatory program; their curriculum/calendar-driven time perspective; their classrooms in which teacher questioning swamps student questioning; their classrooms in which imparting knowledge-facts makes eliciting student motivation a rarity, in which the pressures to conform inhibit any tendency to express personal opinion, pressures no less effective in regard to teachers in their relationships with their administrative superiors.

Some readers will say that what I have said is overdrawn. To say that it is overdrawn is not to say it is wrong. It may be overdrawn but it is not wrong, and I am by no means the first person to come to these conclusions. A foreign visiting friend said to me, "It makes no difference where in America you see and go into a Wendy's, a MacDonald's, or a Burger King. They not only look alike, but you can predict the behavior of everyone in them." In principle that is what John Goodlad (1984) concluded in *A Place Called School* based on a heroic study of many schools representative of schools in general. And that is what the initiators of the eight-year study concluded over sixty years ago. And that was a major theme in Larry Cuban's (1984) classic *How Teachers Taught.*

I am reminded here of John Gunther's (1936) book *Inside Europe*. In his chapter on Nazi Germany he says that the situation there is serious but not hopeless. In the next chapter on Austria he says that the situation there is hopeless but not serious. As a system for education our schools, *as they are now organized and governed,* are both hopeless and serious. They are and will be intractable to improvement. That brings me to the second question.

How did it come about that educators and the general public used test scores as *the* criterion, the overarching criterion, for judging the effectiveness of schooling? Why is it that when test scores began their decline, blame assignment became a cottage industry? Almost any "reasonable" suggestion that gave promise of elevating test scores was tried, and the number of those suggestions was legion, including changing or constructing new tests so that they better measured what students had or should have learned. It was regarded as self-evident that there had to be a measuring rod for evaluation. After all, how can you evaluate without a measuring rod? You just cannot hand a student a high school diploma unless he or she has gotten test scores indicating that the student met an agreed-upon measured standard. Tests were means for measuring knowledge learned in school. Learning that knowledge was the purpose of formal schooling; tests were *the* form of quality control about knowledge learned and academic skills acquired.

Before going on I feel compelled to assure the reader that I am no mindless critic of tests. Given their purposes and awesome responsibilities, schools must use some reliable and valid means for evaluation. The issue for me is not whether the decline in test scores is to be accepted or believed. I accept and believe them as measures of knowledge learned and academic skills acquired. I also accept them as valid indicators of the failure of reform efforts to improve the amount of knowledge learned and skills acquired. And that is the point: are the failures of the reform efforts attributable to the failure to question whether knowledge learned and academic skills acquired is *the* most important purpose of schooling? Is it possible that there is another purpose that if ignored sets drastic limits to achieving other purposes? If so, should we not reexamine why we are so wedded to tests that rather well measure knowledge learned and skills acquired? Should we not stop taking potshots at tests and test makers who are giving us what we ask of them? This is not to say that what we ask of them is unimportant. Knowledge learned and skills acquired are important. But what if what we ask of them ignores a purpose that if not achieved guarantees that our present purposes are unattainable? Yes, I am saying that we have met the enemy, and it is not the tests but us, our inability to take seriously a purpose we know is the most important of all over the course of our lives.

In recent years I have met with a variety of parent, teacher, and school administrator groups. With each of them I asked the following question: "If at the point of a gun you were forced to state the one characteristic you want your child to have when he or she is graduated from high school, what would it be? I know that there is more than one important characteristic you want your child to possess, but is there one overarching one?" That, it turns out, was a difficult question, not because anyone said it was not an important one but because they had not, as one person said, "ever had to prioritize purposes of schooling. Before you asked the question I could have listed three or four major goals I want my children to reach, but I never had to choose among them. I do not feel I can choose one as more important than the others. I trust you will not pull the trigger." (I felt sympathy for that person because it took me years before I could ask that question of myself, let alone answer it to my satisfaction.) Because these meetings had agendas and time was limited I would break the silences by giving my answer: "If when a child is graduated from high school that child is motivated to learn more about self and the world, then I would say that schooling has achieved its overarching purpose. Put in another way, the student knows that the more you know the more you need to know. When I say 'motivated to learn' I refer to that individual's curiosity about his or her interests and talents and where and how they can be tested and exploited in a world not of their making but a world they know they have to comprehend. And that should be as true for the student who is not college bound as it is for those who are. To want to continue to explore, to find answers to personally meaningful questions, issues, and possibilities is the most important purpose of schooling. When that kind of motivation is absent, then knowledge learned and academic skills acquired are not only empty of meaning but devoid of motivational power. To learn because you *have* to is one thing; to learn because you *want* to is quite another thing. And that is my overarching criterion: school is a place a very young child enters with awe, curiosities, expectations, questions, and the desire to feel competent and recognized, and that young child should have those personal characteristics when he or she finishes formal schooling. For those characteristics to be extinguished, to go underground, to get expressed primarily in fantasy is to impoverish a lifetime."

That is both an answer and a minispeech. What I have found so encouraging is that no member of any of the groups who heard my answer disagreed with me, and I do not think I am deluding myself when I say that their agreement was not a way of pleasing a visitor, a Yale professor, a passionate old man. I shall assume that most readers will also be in agreement with my overarching criterion, keeping in mind that there are other important purposes we expect schools to accomplish. So, if you accept what I say is the most important purpose, what follows, what does it mean for action and change? Is that purpose as I have stated it is so laudable, so unobjectionable, as to compel assent without requiring us to confront the chasm between what we believe and the way things are? Let me reconstruct an interchange that took place on one of these occasions between me and a middle school history teacher. (It really was between me, the history teacher, and a high school math teacher, but since the two teachers asked and said essentially the same things, it makes the reconstruction easier if I report it as a dyadic interchange.)

Teacher: I get the feeling that you are implying more than you are saying. For example, are you implying that if a student is learning what we expect him or her to learn but you don't get the feeling that the student is all that interested in learning, then we haven't done our job?

SBS: That's a fair question and I will answer it. But may I first ask you this question: as a middle school teacher you probably have five or six different groups in the course of a day; that is, you teach a lot of kids. How many of them are there about whom you could say they are truly interested in your subject matter?

Teacher: That's why I am asking the question. There is only a handful about whom I can truly say really, obviously like history; the others are there. With few exceptions they do acceptable work, but I cannot say they are interested. In fact, I've given up expecting them to be interested. Does that mean I'm short-changing them? If you say that, then you would have to say that about almost all teachers in my school because they feel exactly the way I do.

SBS: Let's leave blame aside for a moment. Are you aware that there have been studies clearly indicating that, generally speaking, students do not find schools to be interesting places and that you and your colleagues are by no means alone in wishing that students would be more interested in what they are being taught?

Teacher: No, although from what I have read in magazines and Sunday supplement articles, I would say that you are accurate. And, to be completely honest, my own two children in high school complain about being bored in school.

SBS: Would you say they are bored at home?

Teacher: Definitely not. If we did not insist that they do their homework before they do anything else, they would be into this or that, spend hours on the telephone, go here or there, or watch TV. In fact, about the only thing they find boring is going to family gatherings.

SBS: How do you account for the difference between how they experience school and home?

Teacher: I'd really have to think about that.

SBS: I've been thinking about it a long time. May I try out my formulation on you and others in this room? In their activities outside of school they are initiators; those activities express in some way their interests, needs, curiosities; they feel in control; they feel competent; they are exploring themselves, others, and their world. Put it this way: psychologically speaking they *own* those experiences because they make concrete sense to them. They don't own their school experiences in those ways. In school they are passive, not active, learners; reactors, not initiators; impersonal, not personal; question answerers, not question askers; conformers, not individualists; not individuals but part of a category called students; not individuals with assets but individuals with the deficits of ignorance; regurgitators, not articulators; reproducers, not producers.

Teacher: Wow! You are really down on schools!

SBS: No. I am not down on schools the way I am down on crime, pornography, and racial, religious, or gender discrimination, that is, people who know well that what they are doing is judged wrong by society. Our schools are not uninteresting places because people will that they should be that way. There is no malicious intent. What I am down on is our—and I use that pronoun to mean people generally—inability to recognize that we have an asset we do not exploit. And that asset is that we know damned well when and why we have had a productive learning experience, which is followed by the feeling that we know more about ourselves and our world. That is an asset, but you would never know it from the way our schools are structured, organized, and run.

Teacher: So what do we do? What do you recommend?

SBS: (with a feeble attempt at a smile) *Tonight* the issue is not what do we do but that we agree that our schools are based on a conception of learning that guarantees that that learning will be unproductive. Once there is that agreement, once we believe it in a truly gut sense, we will be able to begin to use the asset we all have. And then, and only then, will you be able to answer *for yourself* the question you asked earlier: if students pass "normally" through the grades but with little or no indication that they are interested in learning—they learn because they have to not because they want to—does that mean we haven't done our job? My answer is not that you haven't done your job but that *we*, in and out of schools, have not done our job.

Unless my memory is completely out of whack, or my capacity to fool myself is greater than I think it is, I would like to offer conclusions derived from hundreds of responses of adults to questions I asked about their experiences in schools. More specifically, they were responses to the open-ended question, How would you describe your experience in schools? It was rare for anyone to describe their experience as enjoyable, interesting, or recalled with nostalgia. What was very frequent, indeed near universal, was that these adults could name one, but no more than two, teachers who influenced them in positive ways. Those ways were of two sorts. The first, very small in number, was hearing a teacher say something that sparked the person's interests or curiosity, either because what the teacher said was so strikingly novel or because it contradicted what the student believed. Here is an example that stands out in my mind:

It was during the civil rights upheavals in the sixties, and, of course, I heard a lot about it at home and on TV. Needless to say, I was all for civil rights and against discrimination, and against everything slavery had produced. But very little of what was going on ever really got discussed in our classes even though my high school then had about 25 percent black students. One day in history class Mr. Merriam said that the Civil War did *not* start over the issue of freeing the slaves but rather over whether states had the right to secede from the union [emphasis his]. That floored me, really floored me, and I thought Mr. Merriam, who was an old man, had gone off his rocker. How could he say something so palpably wrong? I told it to my parents that night as an example of why going to school was a waste of time. They told me I probably heard wrong. So the next day I uncharacteristically screwed up my courage and asked Mr. Merriam if he meant what he had said. Mr. Merriam, a gentleman WASP if ever there was one, politely told me that what he had said was a historical and legal fact: the Civil War did not start because the South would not free the slaves. We talked for about ten minutes. Although I have no memory for what he said, I knew he was right. I don't think I ever again felt so humble and stupid. I even went to the library and read about the Civil War in the *Encyclopaedia Britannica*. That is when I became interested in the law, and that was the experience that started me thinking about becoming a lawyer, a civil rights lawyer, of course. For about a week I asked all of my friends why the Civil War started, and when they gave me the answer I had always given, I paraded my new-found knowledge before them with the appropriate professional certainty.

The second category of response, the most frequent by far, is also easier to summarize in this way: "That teacher took a special interest in *me*; I knew she was aware of *me*; she would go out of her way to talk to *me*, to encourage, or to help, or to support *me*. In her class I did not feel I was *anyone*; I was a *me* she wanted and liked to know. I felt *special*. I could trust *myself* to be *me* with her." It is obvious that the words I italicize are to emphasize that what these people were saying was that they felt their *individuality* was recognized;

that teacher not only recognized their individuality but encouraged and supported it; it was not a sometime thing.

Why could these adults recall only one or two such teachers? When I have presented these "data" and conclusions to educators, I have gotten one reaction and one explanation. The reaction is a combination of defensiveness and guilt, as if what I presented was in the spirit of criticism. My denial would not get very far. I could then count on someone to ask what did I think my "data" meant? Before answering that question I would confront them—and it was a confrontation—that *no one seemed to be denying that they did not treat each child in their class as a unique individual different from all others in that classroom.* I was absolutely certain, I would say, that they knew *some* children the way my adult interviewees had described one or two of their teachers. And that was my point: they did not know the bulk of their students in that "special" way. And, I would continue, that is blatantly the case with middle and high school teachers who in the course of a day may have several scores of students.

What explanation did teachers proffer? In each group, and aside from the occasional teacher who regarded me as an Ivy League, armchair, professorial spoilsport (or worse), the explanation was quite simple: "Given the different subject matter grounds we have to cover, there is no *time* to get to know each child's interests, curiosities, needs, and problems. Sure, it would be nice *really* to get to know each student in a personal way, to get from them what turns them on and off, to *really* teach children and not subject matter, but that takes *time* that we simply don't have. Maybe in an ideal school, but we do not teach in ideal schools."

No, schools as they are do not approach the ideal; they are demonstrably counterproductive in regard to what I called the overarching purpose of schooling: to give expression to, to capitalize on, to nurture individuality in learning, to exploit that individuality for its motivational, propelling, cognitive properties. Unless, of course, you do not accept that purpose as the overarching one, in which case you will go along with the tinkering of the present and past, inspired by this or that new educational medicine, disillusioned by its inevitable, paltry consequences, directing blame now to this group and then that group, and, if fortunate, still capable of hoping that there must be a way that schools as we know them can be discernibly improved. The actuarial odds are all against you, and it is unlikely that there will be divine intervention.

Is it not possible, some might argue, that if we *dramatically* reduced class size, teachers would have the time to act more consistently and appropriately in accord with the overarching criterion? Maybe yes, maybe no, but I tend to the maybe no because the question erroneously assumes (or implies) that the preparation of teachers adequately provides them with a basis for how to think about and act in accord with the overarching purpose. And if anything is clear it is that preparatory programs are utterly inappropriate in regard to that purpose. I devoted an entire book (Sarason, 1993a) to why that is the case. What these programs do well is prepare teachers for schools as they are now, not as they should be if they were in accord with the overarching purpose. As I indicate in my book, teachers teach the way they have been taught, which is why I would not have high expectations of a dramatic decrease in class size, although I would be heartily in favor of such a decrease (just as I was in favor of Head Start when it was initiated even though I publicly said that its impact and consequences would not be great).

When we say that we want children to learn, we imply more than our words denote. What we imply is that we want that learning to be productive, to reinforce the desire to learn more. For learning to be productive it has to be in a context alert to and supportive of manifestations of the individual's desire to explore, to master, to incorporate, psychologically to "own" the fruits of his or her efforts. We see this most clearly in the very young child fascinated, puzzled, and drawn to people and the world around him or her. Indeed, we sometimes wish that child would not want to explore, to be into, to do and to "own" everything. As parents we hear ourselves saying that "we can't keep up with the child" for whom the world is busting out all over. We "follow" the child, which is not to say that we do not "lead" the child. We lead the child but only *after* we pay heed to where the child is taking himself or herself. We are not mindlessly permissive—not everything goes—we are unconditionally supportive. We have moral sensibilities and values, but we do not *dictate* them because we know that dictating can win you the battle and lose you the war. We know that our task is to help the child to incorporate those values because that child wants to and not because he or she is forced to. We want the child to regard those sensibilities as his or hers, not only as our sensibilities, not as alien to his or her self-regard.

The fact is that as parents we inevitably fall short of the mark either because of our imperfections or because we live in contexts that have unpredictable and uncontrollable features. (So what else is new?) But at the least we hope that parents know the importance of respecting a child's individuality, of knowing the obligations of following and leading, of "bringing out" and not "pouring in." There are, of course, parents who are insensitive to the child's individuality, whose conception of productive learning is virtually nonexistent, who in principle regard the child as they do their pet animal: something to be "tamed" or "housebroken." Of course they love their child but, as the saying goes, love is not enough.

What I have been saying about parents and the preschool child holds for schools and students. Parents and educators are in agreement, on the level of rhetoric, about respecting individuality. I say on the level of rhetoric because educators, generally speaking, well know that the governance, structure, and traditions of schools, plus the inadequacies of preparatory programs, make respecting individuality impossible. We are not in the mess we are in because of the laws of chance but because pedagogy for respecting individuality *never* has been an overarching purpose of schools. If it had been, we would have schools (and preparatory programs) dramatically different than they became and are. If we understand why, given our national history in the nineteenth century (immigration), schools became what they still are, and we can even be sympathetic to those who had to deal with the realities of those times, let us have the courage and candor to say out loud that we can no longer afford to accept schools where the overarching purpose is not and *cannot* be realized. Today we are dealing with social realities no less thorny and no less potentially destabilizing than those the society faced when schooling became compulsory. What will it take for educators and the general public to realize that, in the case of schools, we "inherited" an institution the features of which doom us to disillusionment and worse? When will we own up to the most obvious feature of schools and preparatory programs in the post–World War II era: their intractability to change in accord with what we say should be their overarching purpose?

As I have in previous books, I must remind the reader that at the beginning of this century the inadequacies of medical education were probably greater than those of our schools today. You may find that hard to believe, in which case I urge you to read Abraham Flexner's ([1910] 1960) report *Medical Education in the United States and Canada*. The significance and impact of that report is hard to exaggerate. If I had to sum up (in my words) in several sentences what Flexner said, it would go like this: "Musicians say that the Beethoven Violin Concerto is not for the violin, it is against it. Medical schools are not and cannot be for the development of physicians who can think but are against it. Given how they are organized and run, they are incapable of improvement. We cannot afford to tinker, to work within their present structures and purposes. If we really want physicians who are knowledgeable and thoughtful, a very different kind of medical school will have to be envisioned and developed, and I (Flexner) will outline what that medical school should look like and in reality be." Medical education was transformed, bearing little similarity to the deplorable, semiscandalous state of affairs it had been.

Dr. Emory Cowen, whose research in schools is like an oasis in the desert, found the following in his mailbox at the University of

Rochester. The unknown author summarizes almost all of the major points I have made in several books; it obviously says a good deal about professorial long-windedness.

Horse Story

Common advice from knowledgeable horse trainers includes the adage, *"If the horse you're riding dies, get off."* Seems simple enough, yet, in the education business we don't always follow that advice. Instead, we often choose from an array of alternatives which include:

1. Buying a stronger whip.

2. Trying a new bit or bridle.

3. Switching riders.

4. Moving the horse to a new location.

5. Riding the horse for longer periods of time.

6. Saying things like, *"This is the way we've always ridden this horse."*

7. Appointing a committee to study the horse.

8. Arranging to visit other sites where they ride dead horses efficiently.

9. Increasing the standards for riding dead horses.

10. Creating a test for measuring our riding ability.

11. Comparing how we're riding now with how we did ten or twenty years ago.

12. Complaining about the state of horses these days.

13. Coming up with new styles of riding.

14. Blaming the horse's parents. The problem is often in the breeding.

15. Tightening the cinch.

As I was writing this chapter the *Hartford Courant* carried news articles about the serious consideration the city's board of education was giving to contracting out the *entire* school system to a private corporation, the same (I think) company that had been entrusted to run several Baltimore schools. There are other examples around the country, and there is no reason to believe that only a few boards are giving thought to such proposals. Basic to such proposals are three assumptions. Schools and school systems are inefficiently and counterproductively run; that is, the structure of schools is OK—they are simply not being correctly administered. The problem is not money; indeed, the private company expects to earn a profit. From my standpoint those two assumptions in no way disconfirm the wisdom in the Horse Story. But there is a third assumption, and that is that schools have not exploited modern technology so as to increase student interest and performance. That assumption has the virtue of recognizing that student interest in school learning is alarmingly low. And by modern technology is meant, of course, putting computers in classrooms. Computers are the new panaceas, the silver bullet that will engage and propel the student not only to learn what society wants students to learn but (presumably) also to allow them to get answers to questions meaningful to *them*, not only questions teachers pose to them. That assumption, especially the part that suggests "individuality," would appear to disconfirm the Horse Story.

It so happens that back in the fifties I had the opportunity systematically to observe the introduction of *talking* computers in the early grades in a private school. I had no doubt then (as I do not have now) that computers are fascinating to students, not all but almost all students. Why? Was it because it literally told them when they were right or wrong, and if they were wrong it did not engender a feeling of stupidity as frequently happens when you give a wrong answer in front of a teacher and a class? Was it that they could proceed at their own pace? Was it the satisfaction associated with the sense of learning what needed to be learned? Was the content of that learning a stimulus to want to learn more? The answer to each question was, in my opinion, in the affirmative. But (there is always a but) it seemed obvious to me that far more important than anything these questions suggested was the child's sense of control over, mastery of, the machine. I did not get the feeling that the content being learned was fascinating or gripping in any intrinsic sense, although it would be unjustified to say that sense was absent. The imagery that comes to mind when I replay my observations is that of the child who successfully takes his or her first steps: The "look, Ma, I'm dancing" facial expression, although it really was as if the child is saying, "Holy cow, *I, I, I* am finally doing it," the sense of competence as a result of *self*-initiated action. I watched several children once a week over a period of several weeks. They did learn what the technology had been programmed to help them learn. But there was also no doubt that once they had mastered the technology they did not approach the talking machine with anything resembling the curiosity-eagerness I observed in my initial visits. And the reason, I had to conclude, was that they were not learning what they wanted to learn but what they had to learn, and whatever sense of mastery they experienced, and I assume that sense was not totally absent, was not much in evidence. I in no way derogate learning what one has to learn. I do thank God for big favors. But let us not forget for a moment that the number of students who do not want to learn what they have to learn is somewhat staggering, and foremost among the reasons is that what they have to learn may have little or no meaning for their interests, curiosities, desires, life context, criteria for utility—in short, their individual selves. Do not confuse the surface appearance of the passive, uninvolved, even somnolent student in the classroom—the student who appears unable or unwilling to think—with what is going on in his or her head. How many times have you sat through a lecture in college with your mind elsewhere? For most students in our schools the times are many, and for some it is continuous, not just now and then.

Despite the fact that the talking computer was heralded as a breakthrough, it was more a fall-down. It went nowhere, and I do not fully understand why, unless because it required that each child have his or her own soundproof cubicle, and that kind of respect for individuality was considered economically unfeasible. We have had a surfeit in education of breakthroughs that fell down, but, to me at least, the talking machine seemed to have promise, despite the limitations I observed.

But that was in the fifties when computers were in their infancy, although there was no doubt in the minds of their proponents that computers would revolutionize the world, and not least our schools. I have friends and colleagues—and I do read—who assure me that today's computers are to the earlier ones as a jet plane is to the contraption the Wright brothers flew. As one of my knowledgeable friends said, "The information highway is being paved—part of it is already done. You have seen nothing yet." If I did not respond with enthusiasm, it was for two reasons. For one thing, the word *information* suggests to me a concept of learning—pouring facts into students—quite congenial to the way most students are taught, *the* way that has contributed to the poor performance of students. But there was another reason for my lack of enthusiasm. In the past several years I have had opportunity to observe the use of computers in classrooms, not a lot of classrooms but several in each of four schools in different parts of the country. With that limitation in mind, I have to report that what I observed I consider a charade and a disaster. To say that the computer programs were stimulating, captivating, or even mildly interesting to students would be totally unjustified. Yes, they liked the computer, but there was no basis for saying that what was on the computer screen in any way "hooked" them. What the computer programs reminded me of was the "Oh, oh, Puff Puff" first grade books of earlier decades. And if I was unenthusiastic, so were most of the teachers, one of whom said (in a whisper), "I do not know what the shouting is all about in regard to the wonders of these computers. *Besides, we were told that we would have and have to use computers. We did not ask for them.*" Perhaps with one or two exceptions these teachers were not what is called "computer literate." When the computers were to be introduced, the teachers went to workshops varying in length from three days to a week. Apparently, those workshops were as helpful as those given in the sixties when the new math disaster took place.

Thou shalt use computers! That commandment, like the ones in the sixties, typifies how change in school is introduced. It is the top-down, fall-down theory of change. A decision is made on the Mount Sinai of the school structure by the board of education and the Moses-Superintendent, and the golden calf will be destroyed! It is as simple, obvious and utterly self-defeating as that.

Computer technology does have enormous, positive possibilities for education. For what purposes? Are all purposes coequally important? On what basis do we decide where on a priority list a purpose should be (which is not to suggest that you downplay, let alone ignore, purposes not at the top of your list)? In this chapter I have argued that at the top of my list of purposes of schooling is to recognize, respect, nurture, and exploit what children are before they enter school: curious, questing, question-asking, competence-seeking *individuals* in search of an identity that propels them to want to learn more about themselves, others, and their world, to want to experience that sense of growth or change, that sense of self-worth without which daily living is literally unproductive; it is routinized, aimless existence, a prelude to a similar future, to an unexamined life. To some ears that will sound flowery, lofty, idealistic, utopian, soupy, and sentimental. If I were capable of stating that purpose in language that students in our schools would understand, I would get unanimous assent just as I would get a thundering no to the question, Is that a purpose you feel your schooling helps you realize?

Ideals *are* ideas about what *should* be; at the same time we know and regret that we will fall short of the mark. It is one thing to aim and fall short of the mark; it is inexcusable if knowing you will inevitably fall short of the mark, you do not even take aim. In regard to the overarching purpose I have stated, we have hardly taken aim even though we know that in our individual lives that is the purpose we want to experience and realize. Even if what I have said is taken seriously, schools will fall short of the mark, if only because too many parents fall short of the mark either out of ignorance or life circumstances antithetical to the recognition and support of a child's individual perspectives and needs. I am quite aware that we live in a real world where there are no magic wands or perfect solutions. In the realm of social-institutional living we are never dealing with problems that have a once-and-for-all solution. They are problems we have to deal with again and again and again. That is all the more reason that we have to become clear about our purposes and direct our aim to an overarching purpose we know will make realizing other purposes more likely.

There are people in and out of the educational arena who proclaim the necessity of "returning to the basics," by which they mean reading, writing, arithmetic, and the world of factual knowledge. To argue against learning the "basics" is truly to be for sin and against virtue and motherhood, leaving patriotism aside. These people are very well intentioned. They are also ignorant of what the public schools have always been: a place where drill in the basics takes precedence over everything else, including the interests, motivations, curiosities of students who would rather be elsewhere. By advocating more time for the basics—or lengthening the school year—they will make a bad situation worse. They are in principle akin to the parent who wakes up one morning and decides that her child is going to be toilet trained, proceeds determined to succeed by next week or the week thereafter, and then does not understand why she has a battle on her hands. In the classroom it has been called "the page 72 syndrome": "by November 1 we *must* be on page 72 in the book." With advocates like that education need never fear for the lack of enemies.

I sound harsh. I do not intend to sound that way, but if it does sound that way, it stems from a feeling of desperation derived from the perception of numerous outcroppings suggesting that people are beginning to accommodate to the possibility that the demise of the public schools may not be such a bad idea. They feel that since reform efforts have failed, that schools as they are have been intractable to change, we should seriously consider alternatives, such as privatization or vouchers, alternatives we think we know how to handle. And that is the point: we define the problem in ways that allow us to think we know what should be done and gloss over the possibility that we are avoiding doing what needs to be done. What I am trying to say is captured in the joke about the man who is ill, in midwinter, and goes to his physician. He receives a thorough examination and then is told to go home, take off all his clothes, open all windows, stand in front of a window, and breathe deeply for a half hour. To which the aghast man says, "But if I do that I will get pneumonia." To which the physician replies, "*That* is something about which I know what to do."

I should remind the reader why I wrote this chapter. Earlier in this book I argued that the existing governance structure of our schools should be abolished and replaced with one less likely to be as productive of problems or as effective an obstacle to much-needed change. In several places in that argument I emphasized that however important and necessary those changes in structure, organization, and power relationships were, the benefits from those changes would be drastically limited unless based on and powered by the overarching purpose I have elaborated on in this chapter. We are used to hearing that form follows function, which is to say that form should reflect purpose. How many buildings are there whose form seems reasonable and even attractive but to those who live and work in them the structures meet the criterion of semi-unlivability? So, if I have convinced some readers that the governance structure of our schools should be changed (i.e., abolished and replaced), I hope they will also agree that unless that change reflects the overarching purpose of schooling, our expectations should not be high. It is obvious, and I do mean obvious, if that purpose powers the change, schools will look and be very different places than they are, which is why some will shrink from examining the consequences and some will say they have no time to fantasize—they are too busy trying to deal with the educational equivalent of pneumonia, the lethal, viral strain.

Chapter Nine

Some Concluding Remarks

It is an old story that teachers recognize and respond to a child's individuality when he or she becomes a problem, that is, when the normal routine or atmosphere in the classroom is disturbed. More correctly, a child may be a walking textbook example of psychological pathology, but unless he or she disrupts in some way the ecology of the classroom, the child is not a social-classroom problem. The passive, or uninvolved, or overtly overly conforming, or underachieving child may be puzzling or frustrating to a teacher, but as long as that child does not disrupt the "governance" or "constitution" of the classroom, that child is not likely to be *formally* labeled as a problem, or that the phenomenology of that child will become an object the teacher seeks to understand. And for two reasons. The first is that the teacher simply does not recognize the plight of that child; there are studies going a long way back in time demonstrating that, generally speaking, teachers are not prepared by their training to recognize and respond to such a child. The second reason is our old "enemy" time; even if the teacher does recognize that something is amiss with that child, responding appropriately to seek understanding takes time. As one teacher said, "I always have at least a handful of kids who should get the attention you are talking about, and I agree with you, but if I did what I think you are suggesting, I would be shortchanging the other students. Not only do I not have the time but I am not a psychologist." The teacher was right. He was not a psychologist. The teacher was wrong in the sense that his conception of a psychologist was that given us by Hollywood movies: someone who understands fully the mysteries of the mind, knows what to say and when to say it, and presto the sources of the individual's problems are revealed, insight is achieved, and the clouds of unhappiness dispensed by the warm sun of understanding.

So much for nonsense. But that conception was one of the most effective barriers to that teacher's recognition that there was a number of actions he could have taken that might have been helpful to the handful of students we were discussing, albeit different actions with different children. I was not suggesting that he put an analytic couch in the classroom. What I was suggesting were nonmysterious ways whereby a child *may* come to feel that he or she is being recognized as the individual he or she is—ways that do not require "extra time"; ways that over time *may* make a difference; ways that for some teachers, unfortunately not many in number, are second nature (i.e., they were that way before they entered a preparatory program and remained so despite it). And that is the point: the individuality of a child, any child, is not something the training of teachers prepares them to recognize and respond to. And by that I do not mean that preparatory programs should produce sophisticated psychologists (whatever that means). I have discussed that at some length elsewhere (Sarason, 1993a). What preparatory programs do is to prepare teachers to organize a classroom, be knowledgeable about how to teach subject matter, and complete a curriculum. Teachers learn to teach subject matter, not children with diverse personality and learning styles.

The teacher was correct, of course, about the pressures on time. But in being correct the teacher was conceding that the goal of schooling "to help each child reach his or her potential" should never be taken seriously.

The preceding scenario is prologue to a current issue that is a predictable consequence of the landmark Education for Handicapped Children Act of 1975, the so-called "mainstreaming" legislation. The issue is illustrative of two things: the culture of the school, and what happens in it when recognition of individuality becomes a possibility. The reader will remember (see Chapter Three) that the legislation contained a procedure requiring that any child labeled as handicapped has to be validly diagnosed, individually discussed in a group of appropriate personnel, an individually tailored program formulated for that child, and meeting the criterion of the "least restrictive alternative." With each year after passage the number of children deemed eligible for services under the legislation increased dramatically, the budgetary consequences of which are obvious. It did not take long before questions began to be raised not only about the budgetary consequences of the yearly increases but also about whether the intent of the law was, at best, being misinterpreted or, at worst, being misused (or both). In the past several years the questions became outcries of criticism contained on the front page of the *New York Times* and other newspapers around the country. Because the legislation required that wherever possible the child with a disability—mentally retarded, or physically disabled, or deaf, or with speech defects, or emotionally disturbed, or learning disabled, or dyslexic—not be segregated from other students, the heterogeneity in the classroom clearly increased as did the resentment of many teachers who had to deal with that heterogeneity. Predictably, the resentment of the teachers centered on the acting-out, difficult-to-manage child who was disruptive.

It is beyond my present purposes to discuss all of the several factors contributing to the steady, seemingly unstoppable increase in eligible children. Nor is it my purpose to suggest that the particular focus of teacher resentment on behaviorally difficult children is totally unjustified. But I do have to say that the number of these children is, relatively speaking, minuscule, and I also want to say, without elaboration, that in my experience (and that of many other people, including school personnel) *some* of these very difficult children (and they *are* very difficult) are as difficult as they are because of teacher personal style, or insensitivity, or lack of flexibility, or psychological obtuseness.

That brings me to Irene Haller in the crumbling, 100-year-old Welch Street School in New Haven where I spent two or three days a week trying to be helpful to teachers. It was a ghetto school in which almost all children were black. It had a handful (no more than that) of behaviorally very difficult children who would drive their teachers up a wall. I intend no criticism whatever when I say that in some of these instances the unmanageability of these children was a clear instance of a mismatch between teacher and child, not unlike what can happen between the personality of parent and child. With one egregious exception, the teachers of these very difficult children were, by conventional criteria, competent teachers. They just could not manage very difficult, classroom-disrupting children, which is to say that they played into and reinforced the behavior they sought to prevent. (None of us is equally effective with every kind of person with whom we have to interact.) Irene Haller, a second grade teacher, could handle these kids quietly, supportively, and effectively as any child therapist I know. She disarmed them; her manner literally was disarming. My problem was that the handful of disruptive children—this was a decade before the 1975 legislation and the use of diverse diagnostic labels—were not second graders. I knew that Irene Haller could manage these children but how could I convince the principal, a no-nonsense, intimidating law-and-order, "shape up or ship out" individual, to transfer such a child to Irene's class? Irene was willing, indeed eager, but the principal was another cup of tea. Between my persistence and the child's disruptions (the latter was much more compelling) these kinds of transfers became possible, indeed necessary. With no exception the disruptive behavior disappeared and not at the expense of learning the "basics," even though these transfers were one or more years older than the children in her classroom. It was that kind of personal experience as well as that of my colleagues at the Yale Psycho-Educational Clinic that permitted us to say that in the case of very disruptive children there was at least one teacher in their school who could manage and teach them well. That conclusion holds only for elementary schools. Middle and high schools are much larger and are organized in ways that make recognition of and adaptation to individuality of students *and* teachers near impossible.

Teachers (and parents) are expected to be equally effective with all of their children and to like-love them equally. That is an expectation we have of no other profession. It is, of course, an outrageously unrealistic expectation, but it is one that many administrators hold, which is to say that they ignore teacher individuality just as so many teachers are insensitive to the individuality of students unless, of course, a student by virtue of behavior forces the teacher to recognize that individuality, which is not to say that they know how to go about seeking to understand and respond to it. As I have repeatedly said (please forgive the repetition), teachers are prepared to deal with *groups* of students, *not individuals*. So, when people take critical aim at teachers, they are "blaming the victim." It is like criticism of physicians for not being as caring and compassionate as they should be, unaware as the critic should be that there is nothing in the selection process of physicians or in their training that bears on the characteristics of caring and compassion. *And the reason most frequently given by physicians is precisely that given by teachers: "I have no time."* It is a reason that concedes the point that recognizing and responding appropriately to individuality is a luxury, an unassailable value or goal that existing realities cannot meet.

Let us return to the question: how do we account for the constantly increasing number of students deemed eligible for individual services under the federal legislation? The answer has at least several major parts. The first is that the legislation *mandated* an individualized assessment and program. The second was that the definition of *handicap* (really plural) lacked, to indulge understatement, precision, unless you equate precision with inkblots. The third was the oft-noted tendency of teachers to seek to get rid of students difficult to understand and manage. And the fourth was the recognition by teachers that some of their students who were *not* difficult to manage needed an understanding and program they could not provide. In brief, the legislation was interpreted and often manipulated—I use that word advisedly—in ways that made it possible for a child to receive individual attention. The floodgates were opened, and that became apparent to me and others not long after the legislation began to be implemented. The point that deserves emphasis is that the steady increase in the number of children deemed eligible spoke volumes about how in general schools are not places where the individuality of a child stands much of a chance to be recognized, dealt with, capitalized on, nurtured, as the case may be.

What I have just said is certainly true in our urban school systems. In the case of suburban school systems the picture is somewhat different because of the pressure exerted by parents to get more individualized attention for their child even if it meant having him or her invalidly and unjustly labeled. If there was a way to get their child with a problem (e.g., a "learning problem") more individualized time, many seized upon that way, sometimes with the "help" of school personnel.

It could be argued that if what I have described is true, even approximately, one could say that we should be grateful that at least the individuality of these children—regardless of whether their labels are justified or not—is recognized, a recognition from which they benefit. Unfortunately, there are no data that would stand up in a court of evidence demonstrating either that individuality has been taken seriously or that the benefits are discernible for other than a few students. If anything is clear in the entire procedure it is that a lot of information is amassed on a child, case folders are not thin, and the program recommended rarely meets criteria for the recognition of individuality.

I give below part of a *New York Times* article (primarily about public schools) that was third in a series ("A Disabilities Program," 1994). The series confirms what I and other observers, in and out of schools, have had to conclude.

Emily Fisher Landau, a member of a wealthy New York City real estate family, had long wanted to create a model educational program for bright youngsters with learning disabilities. Mrs. Landau herself experienced trouble reading as a girl, and it wasn't until she was 56 years old that she was diagnosed as dyslexic.

So a decade ago she chose the Dalton School in Manhattan, one of the pre-eminent private schools in America, to create a Fisher Landau learning disability program.

She donated more than $2 million. Over several years it paid for 14 full- and part-time learning specialists in Dalton's kindergarten-to-third-grade school, a big remedial staff for primary school with 20 head teachers and 400 children. She financed research to develop a screening test that would identify learning disabilities at an early age. And Mrs. Landau gave hundreds of thousands of dollars to Columbia University Teachers College and New York University to evaluate the program and publish scholarly papers, with hopes that the model would be widely replicated.

The outcome of this grand experiment is a cautionary tale about special education. In the last two decades, the learning disabilities field has boomed at both public and private schools, spawning an industry of highly paid specialists who treat loosely defined reading and language problems that no one knows very much about—and that in some cases may not need treatment. Today, virtually everyone at Dalton, including Gardner P. Dunnan, the headmaster, agrees, "things got out of hand."

Dalton's new team of remedial specialists suddenly began finding enormous numbers of bright little children with learning problems. In one three-year period, 77 of 215 Dalton 5-year-olds (36 percent) were labeled "at risk" during their second month of kindergarten and given remedial help. That is far higher than the national rate for learning problems. These were kindergartners with a mean I.Q. of 132, at a school that traditionally sends 40 percent of its seniors to Ivy League colleges.

Parents who just a few months earlier had been proud to have a 5-year-old accepted to Dalton and elated about the youngster's I.Q. score were suddenly being told that a new Fisher Landau screening test indicated "potential visual motor problems" or "sequencing ability deficits."

A learning disability industry grew at Dalton. Instead of being comforted by the school's remedial help, many parents were unnerved and sought even more tutoring and therapy for their children after school from private specialists at a rate of $75 to $200 an hour, said Dr. Gail Furman, the former school psychologist.

By 1992, half of Dalton's students entering fourth grade had already received remedial help. Several Dalton teachers describe their classrooms as being overrun by specialists. One teacher, who had half her class diagnosed with learning problems, says she simply gave up arguing with the specialists and used the Fisher Landau program for her entire class.

Other teachers battled back, refusing to let the specialists in their rooms. When teachers gathered, they joked about how long it would be before the entire primary school was diagnosed with learning disabilities. Jeannie Wang, a former Dalton kindergarten teacher, said: "If you dig hard enough in any kid, you'll find a problem. If you want to have something to write down, you'll find something to write down."

Then, in fall 1992, it abruptly ended. The kindergarten teachers revolted and refused to use the screening test, saying too many children were being given harmful and unreliable labels. Naomi Hill, the new primary school principal with a different educational philosophy, dismantled much of the Fisher Landau program.

Instantly, learning disabilities at Dalton plummeted. This year, half a dozen kindergartners are getting extra help from specialists; about 15 percent in first through third grades receive help.

That such a major shift could occur twice in one place in a decade is a stunning commentary on how subjective the identification of learning disabilities can be and how little is known about them.

Did It Help?

Despite the hundreds of thousands of dollars Mrs. Landau paid the universities, no one today can say with objective certainty whether the remedial program actually helped Dalton students. "We can't answer that question," said Steven Peverly, one of three Columbia researchers who worked four years on the project. "In the field of education there's this problem with research. People don't think about setting up controls. It's not like science."

Even the headmaster, Dr. Dunnan, who continues to call the program "a large success," acknowledges it "was not a carefully controlled bit of research," adding, "it makes the legitimacy of what we did in the research world more suspect."

Getting test scores on children tells me little or next to nothing about what those scores signify for (1) the psychological-social-familial development of the child, how and why the past is in the present, and (2) what that development *concretely* suggests for how relationships should be altered so as to meet that child's individuality. Placing a child in new relationships primarily on the basis of tests may be administratively required but it is psychologically indefensible. And, as the *New York Times* article reminds us, clinical specialists have a bottomless capacity to ferret out deficits and to ignore assets, the hallmark of the anti-individual orientation. These specialists sincerely wish to be helpful (as indeed teachers do) but when you read their reports (as when you observe teachers), you learn little or nothing about how *this* child should be handled in *this* way, in *this* or *that* context by *this* or *that* person. It is like those endless number of commission reports on reforming schools—they say *re*form but they intend no change in structure—that calls for better teachers, but you end up not knowing what they mean by better. And for a good reason: they do not know, or if they do, they are not talking. End of *this* sermon!

This book has had three foci: the moral, conceptual, and practical significance of the political principle; why the existing governance structure of school systems should be abolished; and the question, What is *the* most important purpose by which schooling should be judged? If you accept the arguments I have advanced for the first and third foci, it becomes extraordinarily difficult not to accept the second of the three foci. I say that for two reasons. The first is that the implications of the first and third foci for what a classroom and a school should be are radically different than the rationale for what classrooms and schools now are. The second reason is that the existing governance structure has literally proved that it is incapable of initiating and sustaining other than cosmetic changes; that is, schools have been *intractable* to change. Yes, I (and you) can point to this or that school where the first and third foci have been taken seriously. Neither I nor you can point to a school *system* about which you can say that. The isolated instances to which we can point—and they are very isolated—are what they are not because of the system but despite it, *and in some of these instances they will remain what they are only as long as their personnel remain on the scene.* The system in which they are embedded is simply and obviously not powered by anything resembling the first and third foci. You cannot make a silk purse out of a sow's ear, which reminds me of my master's thesis for which I gave psychological tests to children with very high IQs. I was giving the Stanford-Binet to a ten-year-old boy who appeared to be going through the ceiling of the test. At one of the upper reaches of the scale were "comprehension" items, one of which was: "What does this mean: You cannot make a silk purse out of a sow's ear." To which this boy replied, "They have already done it at MIT." Yes, there are isolated instances, the exception that establishes no rule except the one that says that there are places where individuals and groups have the imagination and courage to do wondrous things because the "system" not only permits but encourages it.

A colleague of mine who read this book (all but this chapter) in manuscript said, "I would have started out by asking the reader, as you have in other of your books, what they mean by productive thinking, its cognitive characteristics and the contexts that stimulate and sustain them, what I think you mean when you say a child should *want* to learn more and more. Then I would have summarized what scads of studies have demonstrated on these points. Would that not have forced the reader to own up to the obvious fact that those contexts simply do not and cannot exist in the way schools have been and are organized and run? It is an open-and-shut case. I agree with you on the political principle, but I would not have started with it because it does not bear directly on productive thinking, which is really what you are after." That gave me pause, and not only because the thought of reorganizing this book was more than I could tolerate. Why did I start with the political principle? It did not take much soul searching—I am not that unknown to myself—to get the answer. In terms of human degradation, war, murderous dictatorships, and lesser forms of man's inhumanity to man, this may be the worst century in human history. I have lived through most of it. If it has not been easy, if there have been countless times I have been tempted to throw in the towel and give up on the human race, I took solace from the fact that at the core of these dispiriting events was the question: did *individuals* have rights and interests that should be respected in ways that allowed them to feel that they literally had some kind of voice, that they could represent those rights and interests even though it meant that their views *may* not prevail? When we accord respect to an individual's rights and interests, should we not expect that we will hear things we do not want to hear, that what we hear may conflict with our views, that we will tend to seek ways that violate the spirit of respect? In this century it became all too easy to violate that spirit, and in a large part of the world that violation continues.

What I have just said is painfully true on the stage of world events. But I have never been an actor on that stage. I, like you, am a member of a society where respect for individual rights and interests is embodied in our Constitution, an inheritance for which we should be eternally grateful. But, as a friend of mine said, that inheritance can also be and has been "one grand pain in the neck." He is a historian who once said to me, "You can write the history of our country as a litany of moral horrors. You can also write it as a glorious history of attempts to protect individual rights and interests. At least in the United States you can write two histories; for most people on this earth there is only one miserable history." The thrust of his remarks was that what happened (and is still happening) on the world stage contains issues with which we in this country are confronted as individuals and organizations. They are not issues only "out there" beyond our borders but "here" as well, albeit getting played out in an infinitely less disastrous way. That is to say, we are not off the hook. Although I have long been committed to the political principle, I confess that its significance for me in the arenas I have worked was not always as clear to me as it should have been. I do not feel guilt about that, I certainly feel more humble, and I have much greater appreciation for those who have difficulty accepting the principle. I am referring specifically, of course, to those in the educational community. That explains only in part why I began this book with a discussion of the political principle. Together with that was my feeling that in regard to our schools we have been and continue to be on a course that is doomed to result in failure, a course with percolating, destabilizing societal consequences. This is not to say that if the political principle is taken seriously, educational outcomes will necessarily be more satisfactory, for reasons I gave earlier. But I strongly believe that those outcomes will be more likely if the existing governance structure is abolished and replaced by one more congenial to the consideration of a reordering of purposes. School systems will not change from within. They will only change in a truly meaningful way when dissatisfaction from within stimulates and coincides with pressures from without. Unfortunately, the dissatisfactions from within our schools have been kept "within" even though more than a few leaders and rank-and-file people know full well that the stultifying features of the governance structure are a mammoth obstacle to the raising and discussion of ideas that challenge that governance structure. Numerous times in earlier pages I emphasized a point both those in and out of the educational community have been unable to perceive: the political principle is violated in the relationships among the layers of the system's hierarchy just as educators violate that principle in their relationships with parents and community, and in both instances the justifications offered are identical.

I started with the political intuitively. That is to say, my entire adult life forced on me the bedrock significance of the political principle in human affairs: personal, social, political, national, and international. What would have surprised me is if I had begun this book with other than a discussion of the political principle. It did not occur to me to start otherwise. From my perspective I was asking the reader "to return to the basics." My colleague was right, except in one respect: what I was really after in this book was to get the reader to accept, in letter and spirit, the legitimacy and wisdom of the political principle. Our founding fathers knew that in 1787, which is why they scrapped the Articles of Confederation and wrote a new Constitution.

A penultimate comment. Bernard Avishai (1994) has written an article with the title "What Is Business's Social Impact?" It is well worth reading. One of the thrusts of the article stems from Avishai's reaction to a visit to a small auto supplier with a reputation for quality:

> The company made fuel injector components and component manufacturing equipment, about $50 million in sales. It was housed in the same square building it had taken over in the 1950s, still looking very much like an oversized garage. But instead of the classical factory scene of lathes spinning or pallets shuttling about, with one man drilling and another grinding, the floor looked more like the operating room of a makeshift hospital, with a scattering of people speaking in quiet tones to one another. The master schedule and customer and quality information were displayed on screens; operators were monitoring them with obvious seriousness. Off to the side was a small room with a glass door, and sitting inside was a lanky blond man wearing a ponytail, moving the mouse on a CAD-CAM system.

A talk with the company's CEO brought its own surprises. "The problem with this country is that the schools don't teach," he said. "I would pay more taxes if people were ready for work. We send a $250,000 machine to a GM plant, and in six weeks it is trashed—it is like sending a Mercedes to Zaire." What of his own company? The problem too is finding people. That young man with the ponytail was at the heart of the company. "Nobody cares about his hair anymore," said the CEO.

This was my introduction to a burgeoning system of production that would change what was meant by the crisis of capitalism. We were entering an age when the problem would not be worker unemployment but rather worker *unemployability* [p. 44].

Having said that it is no surprise that the author goes on to say:

New hires will have to present themselves for work knowing how to keep learning and how to get the best from other people. They will need to speak others' (at times, foreign) languages. They will be undaunted by change and failure. In short, they will integrate to organize the creation of value for customers, using dispersed parts of the value chain [pp. 45–46].

Avishai then discusses and quotes from Ray Marshall and Marc Tucker (1992):

Marshall and Tucker insist that business leaders need to "face the challenge," to acknowledge that public education is worth investing in as a business decision. Next, businesses need to focus on how fit existing schools are for delivering on these goals. Just how should the schools be restructured? Marshall and Tucker borrow heavily from the experience of major U.S. technology companies, suggesting that the schools need to undergo a quality revolution much like the ones led by David Kearns at Xerox and Bob Galvin at Motorola—both of whom, in the authors' view, personify business's enlightened commitment to the reform of public education.

The agenda for reform is ambitious: performance measures, a new curriculum, devolution of authority onto school principals and local administrators, elimination of school board bureaucracy, and the provision of a "whole new set of incentives and accountability measures that provide real rewards for school staff whose students make real progress." In all of these initiatives, business—and Marshall and Tucker really seem to mean big business—would be a kind of activist partner, providing funds for the work of educational foundations, working with community colleges on curriculum, offering a new language of explanation for city school boards (thus, for instance, students are "customers," failing students are "defects"), and even innovating with institutions of higher education of their own.

Schools, feeling the ambient pressure of business, would undergo a quality change something like the one other suppliers to big business have experienced over the past ten years. Companies would present schools boards not with "design specifications"—in other words, the elements of a standard curriculum (read, write, and account)— but with "performance specifications," targets of competence all students must meet. As suppliers, individual schools would take the initiative on how to meet the general standard, while the "customer," the school board, would take the initiative on qualifying the supplier, much like an original equipment manufacturer. Meanwhile, businesses, the next customer in the value chain, would help the school board set appropriate standards: "Many firms would have to help build the science and math curriculum; set technical standards for apprenticeship programs; offer opportunities for on-the-job training; [and] provide mentors, job opportunities and personal support to disadvantaged students" [p. 46].

Avishai does not think that Marshall and Tucker have gone far enough because they are wedded to a notion of education in familiar public classrooms. "When we explode our concept of education to include transforming media and information technologies, both of which are driven by private competitors, the meaning of educational institutions is clearly not going to stay the same." Indeed, he goes on to suggest that our secondary schools, which he describes as "mass-production skill factories," will be a relic of the past.

Some readers, I assume not few, will have reacted to the above as a vision of an Apocalypse where business "finally" controls the education of our youth, molding them to fit in ways that make for "bottom lines" that warm the cockles of the hearts of executives and stockholders. I entreat such readers to set aside that vision, for the moment at least, and try to answer the question, What is the private sector responding to? Is it only simple greed masked by pieties about social responsibility? Is it only ignorance of the "true" purposes of education? Is it another example of science and technology running rampant over issues of values and individual purposes? Is it confirmation of Karl Marx's argument that in a capitalistic society people are objects and things, never fully or partly human?

Before responding to those questions I must tell the reader that in no way will I be suggesting that business (especially the Fortune 500 types) is now composed of leaders lacking in narrow self-interest or now possessed of a semisophisticated understanding of matters educational. What I believe and do suggest is that *some* of these business leaders have learned a good deal about the contexts that make for productive learning, contexts absent in our schools. Let me list some of the things some of them have learned:

1. The adversarial relationship between labor and management, between the layers of the organizational structure, were counterproductive to the overarching goal of being efficient and profitable.

2. The day was past when those at or near the bottom layers would passively accept cipherdom, lack of recognition, lack of worthiness, the role of asset-poor, deficit-rich, dispensable drudges who, like old man river, just kept rolling along.

3. The consequences of points 1 and 2 were intractable to remediation by the traditions, spirit, and letter of the existing governance structure. In almost all of these instances (and it is probably all) they

were sufficiently puzzled, frustrated, and desperate as to seek outside help. Someone said that nothing focuses the mind more than the knowledge that you will be executed tomorrow. These executives saw the equivalent of execution coming down the road.

4. I am making it sound too simple, rational, and cookbookish when I say that two major changes occurred: governance structure changed, and people in all layers of the organization participated *in some way* in planning and decision making. Put in another way, there were now incentives *to want* to learn, change, feel more competent, more necessary to organizational goals. Issues surrounding the allocation and distribution of power decreased in frequency and in untoward consequences.

5. All of the above interacted with the most obvious, change-demanding feature of the modern era: the workplace would be transformed by information technologies for which the existing governance structure and customary personnel relationships were, to say the least, self-defeating. In the abstract, technology is neutral; in practice it challenges, upsets, and exacerbates the messy problem of values, outlooks, the way we define ourselves in relation to others, and how much that we accord to ourselves we should feel obliged to accord to others. If you compare the average workplace before World War II to that of today, it is like comparing apples and oranges (both of which are fruit and that is where the resemblance ends). In the lifetime of current business executives they have learned five things: change is the name of the game, the game seems always to change, learning is a lifetime affair, the alternatives *to wanting to learn* are kinds of living deaths, and the organization that does not create and sustain contexts for productive learning is missing the point and probably the future.

As I said, I am not suggesting that, *generally speaking*, business executives have experienced an "enlightenment" that goes beyond rhetoric and narrow self-interest. That, however, should not obscure the fact that some very influential and articulate business leaders know that the game has changed and should change. The crucial point is that, again generally speaking, business executives, *aware as they are of the changes their organizations have had to make in structure and process, cannot understand why schools have remained what they were and are despite the lack of desirable outcomes.* As one executive said to me, "For a long time American business and industry were based on the stance that if it ain't broke don't fix it. Then we had our comeuppance. It was broke and we had to fix it. Schools are broke and they need to be fixed."

But there is more to their argument. Here is the first paragraph of Avishai's article:

> Our cities are in trouble, and business managers are understandably torn about what to do. They are exhorted to be good corporate citizens and know they command extraordinary resources. Vaguely, managers feel that a once clear separation between public and private sectors has broken down, that they are spending heavily on such things as education and training, and that this may not be their responsibility. At the same time, the financial uncertainties that press on them are stronger than ever before. There are the uncertainties of global competition and new technologies that undermine their sense of command. The new financial industry challenges their governance when the stock price gets even temporarily soft. What, in this context, are business's social responsibilities? Have they changed? [p. 38].

To say that our cities are in trouble may well be the most egregious understatement of the past half century. Later in his paper Avishai, and in one sentence, states what is the source of the most anxiety-arousing concerns in people generally: the problem is less one of unemployment than it is of *unemployability*, a problem whose percolating, destabilizing consequences confront but go far beyond the self-interests of the private sector.

What the reader has to do is to separate Avishai's specific possibilities for transforming schools from the issue of whether he is

correct in concluding that schools must undergo as radical a transformation as business and industry are experiencing. Is he right for
the right reasons or right for the wrong reasons? That he is right I
have no doubt, as I have argued in this and previous books, especially in *Schooling in America: Scapegoat and Salvation* (Sarason,
1983). In fact, in that book I present a cognitive-educational rationale for what Avishai proposes but one that takes explicitly and
seriously the overarching purpose I discussed in the previous chapter—a purpose barely alluded to in his paper. However, slighting
that purpose is one thing, but what is no less troubling is that he
talks *only* about schools, as if what happens in schools is completely
independent of the preparatory programs from which school personnel come. And that is my point: Avishai's diagnosis is very
wrong to the extent that it is woefully incomplete; that is, it com-
mits the error of misplaced emphasis. Of course *schools* are part of
the problem, but so are university preparatory programs, as John
Goodlad has eloquently said countless times. Furthermore, as I read
his paper I found myself expecting that the logic of his argument
would lead him to recommend a dramatic change in governance
structure of our schools. I was disappointed. Essentially, he accepts
the existing governance structure despite his knowledge of the challenges to and changes in the governance structure that the private
sector has and continues to experience.

I had to conclude that Avishai and many "enlightened" executives are do-gooders. I define *do-gooder* as someone who with the
best of motives simply does not know what in hell he or she is getting into. Possessed as they are with rescue fantasies, they enter the
fray armed with good (indeed the best of) intentions only later to
be disarmed by the consequences of their ignorance. *That is true not
only for many in the private sector but for many reformers in the educational community; the former are latecomers to the scene.* So, for example, Avishai says that his proposals would transform secondary
schools. *"Primary schools may well stick to something like classroom-
based teaching, if only to help small children master simple courtesies."* I
confess that when I read that sentence I felt like the man who had

broken several ribs. When a friend asked him how he felt, he replied, "It only hurts when I laugh." With that kind of conception of young children—loveable pets who have to be tamed—the failure of educational reform is guaranteed.

Finally, in earlier chapters I noted that you could find exceptions here and there to generalized criticisms of schools. I bring the reader's attention to one such exception. It is contained in a paper entitled "Enhancing Motivational Opportunity in Elementary Schooling: A Case Study of the Ecology of Principal Leadership" (Butterworth and Weinstein, 1994). I cannot do justice to their description of this school. Here are some of its features:

1. It is a small, K–6, private elementary school with somewhat more than a hundred students. Class size averaged between sixteen and eighteen students.

2. One-third of the students are from relatively poor economic minority backgrounds. The school depends completely on tuition. It is in all respects what has been called an "undermanned setting"; that is, it lacks the financial, spatial, and personnel resources such settings ordinarily have or are expected to have.

3. Precisely because it is such a setting the accomplishment of its educational objectives requires that everyone—teachers, parents, *and* students—perform a variety of functions. The following provides glimpses of what their fuller description contains:

> Admissions to the school were largely non-selective (on a first-come, first-serve basis), except in the case of ensuring ethnic minority representation. An active scholarship program resulted in minority representation in each class at a higher level than its surrounding public school district (approximately 30 percent). An afterschool program also drew single parent and two-worker families from a wide variety of socioeconomic positions. As a result, the

population of children attending the school was as varied as the local public schools. Thus, there are elements in its design that are similar to and can be generalized to the public sector.

In addition to the regular academic program (which differs perhaps by virtue of specialist teaching in the elementary grades and by the requirement of a second language), there existed a variety of additional programs which enhanced the daily classroom activities. These included student government, a school economy, publishing, theater performances, an outdoor education program, community experiences, an afterschool program, and holiday celebrations.

The school had a system of student government in which a mayor, vice-mayor, secretary, treasurer, and social coordinator were elected by the whole school twice a year. Each individual running for office appointed a campaign manager who, along with the candidate, prepared a speech as well. Representatives from each class completed the membership of the governing body. Two teachers helped the students plan activities and fund-raisers for the school.

The school also had an economic system in which children held regular jobs around the school and were paid a weekly salary in the local scrip, keybucks. Jobs ranged from aiding in the classroom or office to maintenance around the school grounds: adults in the school supervised jobs related to their interests and classroom/subject area needs. Jobs were listed, students wrote applications, and were interviewed for positions. Students could save keybucks in the bank (run by the sixth grade) or spend keybucks at the school store (run by the fifth grade) or bookstore (run by the fourth grade) and for field trips and the use of special equipment like computers.

Publishing was a third area of activity for the school. A student newspaper was published monthly, staffed by students from all the grades, and a literary magazine was published twice a year by the fourth grade. A yearbook with photographs was also published by a student staff with teacher help. The principal wrote a weekly Wednesday letter to parents and children and classroom teachers routinely sent home newsletters about class activities.

During the year, two school-wide performances were held, a

musical for the holiday season, and a dramatic or musical comedy at the end of the year. Scripts were modified so that every child in the school performed in the play. In addition, each grade put on a play for the school and for parents.

An outdoor education program involved fourth–sixth graders in a five day camping trip to an area of ecological importance and younger children in one night camping trips. Class visits to community theatre, concerts, and museums were also regular parts of the program. Students brought their own performances to local homes for the aged. Community resources also visited the school, for example, two architects collaborated with fifth grade students in designing a model community for their social studies assignment.

The year was also punctuated by celebration—Halloween parades, Thanksgiving luncheon, Martin Luther King's Birthday, Grandparent Day, Graduation dinner to list a few. These traditions have developed rich, elaborate rituals which brought energy to the school periodically during the year and warmly involved the family community.

Before school opened and after school hours, a rich and varied program was available for children whose families sign them up at an additional cost. Staffed by adults as well as local high school and college students, activities included a study hall for homework, art projects, films, and sports program and leagues with other schools. Signups were for single days or on a regular basis. The afterschool program expanded its hours for school half-day closings when teacher-parent conferences were held [pp. 14–17].

That is what I mean by taking the overarching purpose of schooling seriously. But that is not why I have presented it here; I am sure that there are other exceptions. I presented it to deal with the question: since this is a private school, can its features be replicated in a public school? Part of the answer has already been given in that this was not the kind of school we ordinarily think of as a well-heeled private school containing youngsters only from secure economic backgrounds—witness the fact that it had more minority students than surrounding public schools. What distinctively characterizes this school is its perception and thorough-going *redefinition* of who in the school *and* community were assets and resources for educational purposes. *And that included the children.* Clearly, the school had many important purposes, but, equally, clearly, the overarching one was reinforcing children's *wanting to learn*, as the words in the paper's title (enhancing motivational opportunity) says.

Replicating what happens in one setting in another is literally impossible, a fact the elaboration of which would require another book. You can read the Butterworth and Weinstein paper and point to this or that of the school's features that would make replication difficult, although in my opinion the number of those features would not exceed one, perhaps two. The point is that when people talk of replication, they almost always mean replicating what people *do* (i.e., the overt, describable goings-on). In that sense replication is impossible; it can only be approximated (i.e., things will look and happen differently). What is absolutely crucial in replication is that the assumptions, conceptions, values, and priorities undergirding what you seek to replicate are clear in your head and you take them seriously; you truly accept and believe them; *they are nonnegotiable starting points.* "How to do it" is one thing; "how to think it" is another. One of the things replicators have learned, usually after failure, is that there are minimal conditions that if not met mean that replication stands no chance of even being somewhat approximated. And one of those minimal conditions is that you have thought through and accepted the rationale, the "how to think and believe it" process, to the point where you know what other minimal conditions need to exist if you are to stand a chance of being consistent with that rationale.

The Butterworth and Weinstein rationale is no great mystery. It is a distillation of what has long been known about productive learning, its processes and contexts. They took it seriously and literally created the appropriate contexts. Is this rationale applicable to and replicable in public schools? The answer is yes, it is applicable; the answer is no, it is not replicable given the way our schools are organized and governed. That is not my opinion alone. I asked four elementary school teachers to read the Butterworth and Weinstein paper and to answer the question, "Could this be done in your public school?" They did not laugh in my face, if only because the article reminded them of the gulf between what they had read and what they daily experienced and did. But one of them did say something that plaintively summarized what all of them felt: "Since when are schools places congenial to the vision and persistence of the writers of that article?" Translating it into my words, "Since when have schools been organized and run informed by what we have long known about productive learning?" They have never been so organized and run. Today, however, the societal stakes are much higher than ever before.

References

"Academic Disciplines Increasingly Entwine, Recasting Scholarship." *New York Times*, Mar. 23, 1994.

Avishai, B. "What Is Business's Social Impact?" *Harvard Business Review*, Jan.–Feb. 1994, pp. 40–46.

Butterworth, K., and Weinstein, R. "Enhancing Motivational Opportunity in Elementary Schooling: A Case Study of the Ecology of Principal Leadership." Unpublished paper, Department of Psychology, University of California, Berkeley, 1994.

Concerned Women of America. *Outcome Based Education: Remaking Your Children Through Radical Reform*. Washington, D.C.: Concerned Women of America, n.d.

Cuban, L. *How Teachers Taught*. New York: Teachers College Press, 1984.

"A Disabilities Program That 'Got Out of Hand.'" *New York Times*, Apr. 8, 1994.

"Evaluating (and Defending) Teachers." *New York Times*, Jan. 16, 1994.

Flexner, A. *Medical Education in the United States and Canada*. Washington, D.C.: Science and Health Publications, 1960. (Originally published 1910.)

Freedman, M. *The Kindness of Strangers: Adult Mentors, Urban Youth, and the New Voluntarism*. San Francisco: Jossey-Bass, 1993.

Goodlad, J. *A Place Called School*. New York: McGraw-Hill, 1984.

Goodlad, J. *Educational Renewal*. San Francisco: Jossey-Bass, 1994.

Gunther, J. *Inside Europe*. New York: Harper, 1936.

Holmes, E. "Total Quality for Americans." *Issues and Observations*, 1993, 13(4), 1–6.

"House Bows on Home Schooling." *Arizona Republic*, Feb. 25, 1994, p. 1.

Koch, K. *Wishes, Lies, and Dreams: Teaching Children to Write Poetry*. New York: Chelsea House, 1970.

Marshall, R., and Tucker, M. *Thinking for a Living: Education and the Weather of Nations*. New York: Basic Books, 1992.

Martin, J. H., and Harrison, C. H. *Free to Learn*. Englewood Cliffs, N.J.: Prentice-Hall, 1972.

Meyer, E. (Letter to the editor.) *The Connecticut Post*, March 6, 1994.

"Private Groups to Run 15 Schools in Experiment by Massachusetts." *New York Times*, Mar. 19, 1994, p. A1.

The Report of the Commission on Educational Excellence for Connecticut. Hartford, Conn.: Commission on Educational Excellence for Connecticut, 1994.

Sarason, S. B. *The Culture of the School and the Problem of Change.* (2nd ed.) Boston: Allyn & Bacon, 1982.

Sarason, S. B. *Schooling in America: Scapegoat and Salvation.* New York: Free Press, 1983.

Sarason, S. B. *The Making of an American Psychologist: An Autobiography.* San Francisco: Jossey-Bass, 1988.

Sarason, S. B. *The Predictable Failure of Educational Reform: Can We Change Course Before It's Too Late?* San Francisco: Jossey-Bass, 1990.

Sarason, S. B. *The Case for Change: Rethinking the Preparation of Educators.* San Francisco: Jossey-Bass, 1993a.

Sarason, S. B. *Letters to a Serious Education President.* Newbury Park, Calif.: Corwin, 1993b.

Sarason, S. B., and Klaber, M. "The School as a Social Situation." *Annual Review of Psychology,* 1985, 36, pp. 115–140.

Shanker, A. "The School as a Social Situation." *New York Times,* Mar. 20, 1994.

Trubowitz, S., and others. *When a College Collaborates with a School.* Boston: The Institute for Responsive Education, Boston University, 1984.

Index